Defining the Church for Our Time

Defining the Church for
Our Time

Origin and Structure,
Variety and Viability

Peter Schmiechen

CASCADE *Books* • Eugene, Oregon

DEFINING THE CHURCH FOR OUR TIME
Origin and Structure, Variety and Viability

Cascade Books
An Imprint of Wipf and Stock Publishers
199 W. 8th Ave., Suite 3
Eugene, OR 97401

www.wipfandstock.com

ISBN 13: 978-1-61097-926-9

Cataloging-in-Publication data:

Peter Schmiechen

    Defining the church for our time : origin and structure, variety and vitality / Peter Schmiechen.

    xiv + 170 p. ; 23 cm. —Includes bibliographical references.

    ISBN 13: 978-1-61097-926-9

    1. Church and the world. 2. Christianity—21st Century. I. Title.

BV 600.2 S328 2012

Manufactured in the U.S.A.

To

The Faculty, Staff, Students, and Trustees
of Lancaster Theological Seminary

". . . saints and faithful brothers and sisters in Christ. . . ."
COLOSSIANS 1:2

Table of Contents

Preface

I WENT TO LANCASTER Theological Seminary in 1985, eager to explore the relation of faith to the life and work of churches. I was aware that major changes had been taking place in religion in America involving the new pluralism of world religions, the rise of secularism, the decline of mainline churches, the definition of ministry and the demands placed on pastors. Churches were under tremendous pressure to respond to hot social issues. Whatever congregations or national offices did in response seemed to be divisive. If all this were not enough, it soon became apparent that much of the allure of ministry had disappeared, as reflected in the lower enrollment in mainline seminaries. Equally important were changes in the student profile: fewer men enrolled directly from college, but there was a gradual increase in the number of women, students over thirty, and students from fifteen other denominations. These were drastic changes for seminaries in some twenty-five years, and signaled new challenges for churches. There would be fewer new ordinands and nearly the majority would be women.

In such a situation it was not surprising that proposals for growth in numbers and finances were everywhere. Every great success story generated a new model of ministry and strategy for reorganizing congregations. Some related to rethinking the relation of the church to a pluralistic, secular culture. Others related to special areas of ministry, while others emphasized targeting the younger, unchurched population through new forms of worship and music. For many national leaders and pastors, the demands for social justice were the overwhelming imperative facing the church. If this involved redirecting attention and resources, so be it, even if it meant ignoring traditional programs and forms of ministry.

After several years of working with faculty, students, trustees, and pastors, my interest was drawn to the issue of the church's central message. Amid all the great debates about organizational issues, preaching, worship, music, and stewardship, not much attention was given to the question: What is the message? I sensed that mainline pastors lacked clarity and confidence regarding the message because they were stuck in the middle. On the one hand, conservatives were charging that the mainline was declining because it was soft on the authority of the Bible and preaching the cross. On the other hand, liberals were charging that the traditional view of penal substitution (i.e., Jesus dying to appease an angry God and the demands of the Law), with its patriarchal world view, was totally unacceptable. Most pastors did not like the criticisms or the solutions. While they were not ready to embrace either side, they were not clear about the alternatives. This produced the lack of confidence regarding the message. When that happens, it is not surprising that one turns to matters of form and/or new strategies.

The first question, then, was regarding the message. But it soon became apparent that this question merged with a second: What is the relation of the message to the church? Americans favor liberty over equality and community. They are traditionally suspicious of institutions. They have been raised on the assumption that the basic unit of society is the individual—not communities of nurture and support for the common good. If there must be institutions, then they should exist to carry out specific functions. But institutions do not represent a positive or necessary form of life; rather they are functional devices to do certain things. This bedrock value lies at the basis of the individualism so prevalent in American life. It surfaces in libertarianism, which paradoxically appears in both the Left and the Right. Thus in both political parties one can find the suspicion of government solidifying into the declaration that government is evil.

The suspicion regarding institutions surfaces in contemporary religion in many ways. For starters it helps explain how the message of Jesus is so easily uncoupled from the church. One can be a Christian without going to church or participating in any way. Leaders of churches reflect the same attitude by a willingness to speak of God and morality without asking someone to join the church or give to the church. I have never been in a discussion with pastors regarding evangelism where someone did not make the point that evangelism has nothing to do with numbers of new members. What struck me was not simply that some pastors were sensitive about numbers, but quite unsure about asking someone to join the church. This is not to say these persons were not good pastors. Indeed, when it came to those ministries directed to the members, they were more than faithful. The problem was that in a period of decline, church leaders and pastors were not able to address the issues of evangelism, stewardship, and the calling of new leaders.

I took these trends to be a sign of disinterest in the church as an institution existing in time and space. This has been especially harmful for mainline churches, as they have experienced the greater losses in members, funds, and influence over the past forty years. But the suspicion of institutions also appears among conservative traditions. On the surface it appears in evangelism programs aimed at individuals and their relation to Jesus. But at another level, it appears in an unexpected way. By making claims to an absolute Bible or absolute doctrine, the church as a human community is denied any real significance. Since the answer for every question is already given, one does not have to deal with the complex and messy issues arising out of a new time and place. As with churches in the first century or among the reformers of the sixteenth century, there is no risk or struggle in asking what the gospel means for our time and place. One does not have to construct an inter-generational structure to determine what is the message for a community today because the answers are prescribed in Bible verse, doctrine, or laws. In this sense, the church ceases to be a community struggling at the foot of the cross but becomes the church triumphant where everything is ordered. In such a situation, the absolute claims of Bible and doctrine exempt these churches from the general suspicion regarding institutions. But one can still disregard all other churches as well as the National Council and the World Council of Churches. (One might also note the increasing movement for local conservative churches to re-name themselves without using a traditional denominational name, such as Baptist.)

What we find, then, is that pastors have had to deal with contradictory and confusing attitudes about the message and the church. On one side there are liberal tendencies to disconnect the message from Jesus. This approach is usually wrapped in the language of individualism, suspicion of institutions, and a preference to turn religion into morality. On these terms the church and ministry are defined functionally: they exist to do certain things. One can ignore the needs of the church because churches exist only to support liberal causes. On the other side there are conservative tendencies to confine the message to a problematic view of Jesus (penal substitution) and selected social values, supported by claims to an absolute Bible or absolute doctrine. In this view churches exist to support conservative social values, even though this inevitably leads to legalism and continual divisions. When the call to ministry places one in between such alternatives, it is all the more necessary to ask two questions: What is the message? How is the message related to the church?

It took me several years to reach clarity on these two questions. How I approached them was determined by my work with students, faculty, pastors, and church leaders, as well as my theological studies. Since one of my interests in theology was Christology, it did not take long to begin thinking about the current church situation from the standpoint of the message. After all, Luther had declared that the true treasure of the church was the gospel of Jesus Christ. This prompted a study of the renewal of the church by means of a recovery of the gospel of reconciliation (*Christ the Reconciler: A Theology for Opposites, Differences and Enemies*). The message was placed in the context of the crisis of the church in contemporary America.

Seven years later I decided to explore the message from the perspective of multiple theories of atonement. The purpose was in part historical (i.e., to recover the wide range of interpretations of Jesus) and in part a concern for the renewal of the church (i.e., there can be no confidence about preaching Jesus if one does not have conviction about the cross of Jesus). This study culminated in *Saving Power: Theories of Atonement and Forms of the Church*.

While it can be said that *Saving Power* made the connection between Christology and the church, in that work the discussion of the church took the form of general conclusions. The entire relation of the message to forms of the church needed further development. What drives believers to create different forms of the church? Are the differences essential or accidental, valid or erroneous? And what about the definition of the church itself? If churches are divided and/or at war with one another over all manner of social, moral, and practical matters, how do these matters relate to the definition of the church? These were the questions that prompted my further study of the church. As I progressed the project evolved to include:

- a broader and more inclusive definition of the church.

- a basis for unity in the face of the most serious disagreement.

- a positive explanation for the variety of traditions, namely, that patterns of grace, what I have termed strategies for change, are decisive in the formation of specific churches.

- the marks of vitality for churches in an ecumenical age.

My intention has been to turn the corner from lamenting what is wrong with the church to a positive and constructive affirmation of the church. This means moving beyond criticism but also rejecting the American assumption that institutions are merely functional devices created to do things. I hope the work reflects the strong affirmation of the reality of the new life in Christ present in the church (and of course, in the world). The Mercersburg theology has pointed the way toward the celebration of the church as a sign of a new reality on earth.

This is not to deny that I have for many years grieved for the sufferings of the church, especially the lack of affirmation regarding the total life of the church. It was never my intention to pit so-called institutional needs over against care of people, fellowship, outreach, or social witness. The concern, rather, was to affirm the total life of the church as a community over time. When all of the needs of the church go unmet, the church suffers. As I shall argue, the church is more than worship and sacraments, or worship and the care of members, or even social witness. The problem is that when only a few forms of ministry dominate, forces are set in motion that ultimately threaten the vitality of congregations. We know what happens when buildings are neglected and face deferred maintenance. What we are slow to recognize is how congregations can also suffer from *deferred spiritual maintenance* because key aspects have been neglected, be it preaching, education, evangelism, fellowship, or social witness. I have also grieved the neglect of things directly related to the sustenance of churches: evangelism, stewardship, nurture of candidates for ministry, and support of theological education. The great American heresy is that one can be religious without going to church. Its by-product is that a church can exist without new members or well-educated leaders. Congregations are not self-renewing organizations—especially when they lose most of their children. Nor are they perpetually energized and motivated. They need to hear again and again the good news in worship and preaching; they need the renewal of programs and pastors in concert with regional and national systems of support. They also need to celebrate and affirm the church with a vision of its place in the revealing of God's glory.

I am indebted to many people for sharing ideas and analysis over many years: the faculty, staff, students, and trustees of Lancaster Seminary, as well as pastors, lay leaders, and regional church leaders from many denominations. I have been inspired by their willingness to open their hearts regarding the life and work of the church. It was through the sharing of a common faith and work that new ideas and forms of ministry emerged. In particular I have benefited from programs for the renewal of churches at Lancaster Seminary funded by the Lilly Endowment. Participation in the Mercersburg Society, a community bound together by an ecumenical vision of the church inspired by John Williamson Nevin and Phillip Schaff, has also provided encouragement.The Sunday Morning Adult Class at First Presbyterian Church of Lancaster allowed me to share some of the basic ideas of this study over several weeks. These discussions came at a critical point in the development of the core ideas. I am especially grateful to two conversation partners over many years: Dr. Wayne Glick, former President of Bangor Seminary, and Dr. Lee Barrett, Professor of Theology at Lancaster Seminary. For inspiration and encouragement from many sources I am most grateful.

I also wish to thank staff of Wipf and Stock Publishers for their assistance in moving the manuscript to book form: Christian Amondson, Assistant Managing Editor; Heather Carraher, Lead Production Editor; and Rodney Clapp, Editor.

Peter Schmiechen
Lent, 2012
Lancaster

Introduction

Reforming the Church

THE CHURCH IS BROKE and we cannot fix it. Unless we acknowledge this we will never hear the good news. So let us begin with the recognition of where we are. We live in a world where many people profess belief in God and loyalty to Jesus but no interest in the church. There is caution, if not suspicion, about the church, its symbols and especially its language. For many the authority of the churches is diluted by conflicting claims as well as the abuse of power. The efforts to reclaim authority in the social and political culture wars only reinforces the impression that churches are the backup choir for opposing cultural values. The problem is, to be sure, radical changes in the culture and the role religion plays. But it is also the challenge of making a case for Christian faith in this new world. In such a setting, the older ways of speaking about Christ and the church do not serve us well. Once again the church must be reformed and that includes both the way we proclaim the gospel and the way we think about the church.

The Challenge of Our Times: To Speak with Clear and Certain Words

In my lifetime the religious landscape has changed in radical ways: one was the change from a denominational world to an ecumenical Christian world; the second was the change from a predominately Christian-Jewish perspective to the new pluralism of world religions and secularism. These changes have had tremendous impact upon the general culture as well as the life of churches. Some Protestants have resisted and even denied these changes, in yet another effort to establish a state church in America. Others appear to be working overtime at building authoritarian fortresses to protect themselves from the dangers of a secular world. One group claims an infallible Bible, another an infallible church. At the same time, all churches have discovered that they cannot rely upon support from the culture. They cannot expect new members to walk in the door nor assume that people outside the church will value the church's authority or symbols.

How this affects congregations may be illustrated this way: Most Protestant congregations have functioned as communities of belonging based on loyalty. But since the 1960s two things have affected such communities of loyalty. One is that the bonds of trust in government, business and financial life, families and churches have been violated by illegal actions, dishonest and self-serving practices, as well as infidelity and violence. People who have been let down, cheated or violated withdraw their loyalty and only give it again when it has been earned. The second factor is that several generations of young people have left the church. Instead of being the doorway to adult membership, confirmation has been the exit from the church. Some are alienated from churches because of bad experiences, but most are simply detached, not knowing what to make of organized religion. Since they know little about Christian faith and live in a world where prudential reason prompts one to think of commitments in terms of self interest, they ask: "Why?" Why should they attend, give, serve or join a church? To further confound congregations, they assume these questions will be answered in terms of personal self-interest, not in terms of Scripture or traditional answers.

This exposes the vulnerability of the church as a community of belonging. Communities of loyalty expect people to know why they should join the church, and certainly not expect an answer in terms of their self-interest. When young people and those outside the churches ask "Why?" such a question appears disrespectful, if not disloyal. Did not Jesus tell us to lose ourselves for the gospel? But to press seekers to be loyal without giving a reason is basically another way of trying to make them feel guilty. If we have learned anything about human relations, we ought to know that guilt is hardly an effective strategy for gaining new members. The real problem is that few congregations are prepared to make the case to people who don't share their values or language. In fact, many pastors are terrified at the prospect of such conversations. While they are excellent at caring for the beloved community, they are threatened by the fear of rejection when speaking to outsiders.

This commentary on the crisis within congregations highlights the many ways the new cultural setting requires new responses. How do you proclaim the gospel to a culture that:

1) does not know the language of faith and does not accept the church's norms?

2) speaks the language of personal needs, health, wealth, and success?

3) contains a wide range of people who are alienated from organized religion because of the repressive and authoritarian practices of religion itself?

These concerns emphasize that the language we use will be crucial in defining the church. We cannot assume that listeners know what Biblical images of *covenant* or *Body of Christ* mean. If we are going to invite persons into a new world of Christian life, we will have to speak in clear and certain words. But most of all, these three concerns point to the requirement to answer the question: Why? What is it about the church that gives us the authority and the obligation to invite someone to participate in it? In a culture where religion is too often defined in terms of my interests and needs, why should someone consider self-sacrifice and service? This question requires a theological confession which serves as a standard for thinking about the church. What is needed is to reconnect the saving power of God in Jesus Christ with the community of Christ on earth.

Moving Beyond the Traditional Approach

Traditional discussions of the church tend to focus on the origin of the church. So, for example, we find references to incarnation and resurrection, the Body of Christ, the vine and branches, rebirth in the Spirit and the Pauline image of life *in Christ*. Attention is given to the nature of our union with Christ, as expressed by the classic marks of the church, namely, that the church is one, holy, catholic, and apostolic. Norms for governing thought and practice are usually drawn from a golden age of the church (be it the early church, the Reformation, the Puritan or Anabaptist movements). With these categories in mind, a basic definition of the essence of the church is set forth. What is primary (i.e., Jesus Christ and our union with him) is elevated to the level of essentials; everything else is consider non-essential or secondary (i.e., matters of order, practice, relations to the world, and social/moral issues).

This approach does not serve us well in our current crisis. The problem is not that it is incorrect, but rather incomplete and not helpful. Defining the church is this way does not describe the church's actual life or give us the means to deal with the challenges we face. Let me support this conclusion with two arguments.

DISTINCTIONS THAT ARE NO LONGER APPLICABLE

Let me begin with a story. Some years ago I attended a regional gathering of churches. The group was asked to affirm the Trinity, the Incarnation, the Virgin Birth and a ban on homosexuality. That is indeed a surprising list of priorities. Here were three articles of faith from the creeds now joined with a hotly debated social issue. It prompted me to wonder what other issues from the realm of social/political practice might be added to such a proposal. How many times could we find grounds for dividing the church? But my main concern was what this proposal said about a church's ability to maintain unity in the face of serious differences. In the past, the traditional definition of the church had a very specific answer to this problem: Things relating to God and our life in Christ were considered essentials, whereas everything else was deemed non-essentials. We were raised with the admonition: "In essentials unity, in non-essentials liberty, and in all things charity." The words did in fact keep peace within a congregation or denomination, though too often the peace was maintained by a vow of silence not to speak of all our disagreements. But this way of keeping peace in church families does not work anymore. Everything has become an essential! One view on a social issue is now as important as Trinity, Incarnation, and Virgin Birth. Our toleration for living with serious disagreement, because of a common faith in Christ, appears to be in short supply. Thus everything in that general category called non-essentials has the potential for being considered an essential and, as a consequence, dividing the household of faith.

4

There is something very disturbing about this tendency to make specific concerns a test for the true church. Matters of church order, worship, music, or even moral decisions do not have the same status as the Doctrine of the Trinity. But having said that—and I have said that many times in my travels among churches—let us look at the issue from the opposite perspective. Without naming it, the proposal to merge a specific moral policy with a primary theological article of faith points to a weakness in the traditional way of defining the church. It is the problem of defining the essence of the church in terms of a small set of articles (usually regarding God, Christ, and sacraments) and confining everything else to secondary status. Many of the things pushed to the secondary level are really very important to us—in fact, so important that we think they are essentials. Why is this?

One reason is that the distinction between essentials and non-essentials (or primary vs. secondary matters) creates an unreal division. The church is not simply Jesus Christ and the sacraments, but the community formed by Jesus Christ existing over time in this world. There are many general needs of the community which require serious attention. In fact, many things needed for the journey along the way are essential to the church's life. Let me illustrate this by reference to another realm of experience. I would find it quite inadequate to define an American by pointing to the Declaration of Independence and the Constitution, without reference to anything else. An American is not a pure spirit, disembodied from time and space, who holds certain principles. He or she is a human being with a history, formed by a community of faith, memory, structures, and practices. Americans today have several centuries of history, with only a few assuming that they still live in the eighteenth century. And lest we forget, Americans belong to communities which interact with other communities in the larger world. In a similar way, defining the community that claims Christ as its head must give attention to the total life of the community in time and place.

The point may be made in another way: essentials and non-essentials cannot be easily divided. In the actual life of the community the core values interact and merge with daily life. The so-called essence takes form in the order and practices of the community, just as the community's life begins to shape the essence. Again an illustration: if we gather together a Roman Catholic, a Lutheran, and a Mennonite, do you think they would

---

agree to the proposition that they share a common essence of faith in Jesus Christ and the sacraments, but that everything else is non-essential or accidental? After listening to how they speak of themselves as Christians, we would be more inclined to admit that the so-called essence is embodied in each person's tradition, culture, practices, and communal structures. In effect, the three really are different and the differences cannot simply be ignored as secondary matters. That is why people fight over communal practices. The practices are perceived as being directly tied to the so-called essentials of faith. If this analysis is correct, then we have to admit that in the case of our three Christians, while they may share some commonality between their affirmations of Jesus Christ, the affirmation of Jesus Christ by each still bears the distinct marks of each person's tradition. The essentials cannot be defined in isolation from the life of the community. We are thus forced to admit that if the church is Jesus Christ and the sacraments, in actual cases it is Jesus Christ and the sacraments as confessed and lived out in the day-to-day life of churches.[1]

Yet another way of making the point is to consider that the traditional approach cannot explain why churches differ. If we are all united by a core of universal essentials, why then do we differ? To say our differences are non-essential is to suggest we should not take them so seriously,

1. My disagreement with the traditional approach may well reflect the difference between a rationalist and an historical way of defining subjects. The rationalist view assumes that a definition consists of the logical essence, with historical particulars considered to be secondary or accidental. The real thing is what all particulars have in common. For this reason, the rational perspective shuns an historical approach, since history involves things tied to time and place. The mistake made here, however, is that the logical ideas are considered to be the actual reality, when in fact they are logical or formal definitions abstracted from the reality. By contrast, an historical approach assumes that the so-called common elements only appear in particular forms with their distinctiveness. For example, all human beings may have common anatomical and physiological systems, as illustrated in biology books, but each human being embodies them in a distinctive way. To be sure, the differences may seem small and certain body parts may be interchangeable. But there is no generic human being walking the earth, only specific human beings, differentiated by race, ethnicity, gender, diet, and other factors. Applied to the debate at hand, the practice of talking about the essence of Christianity by naming a short list of essentials is very rationalist, or if one prefers, Modernist. It assumes logical analysis can isolate the essence from historical particulars. Thus, if a Roman Catholic, Lutheran, and Mennonite all affirm Jesus Christ is Lord, then it is assumed that each affirms exactly the same view of Jesus Christ. Whatever is unique to each is considered secondary. By contrast, an historical approach would see the three Christians as distinct forms of Christianity. One can speak of commonalities, but it is not possible to separate the so-called essence from accidents, the primary from the secondary.

or perhaps that we are totally wrong in affirming them at all. This is, of course, one way we have approached differences: my church is right and all the others are wrong. But this has never been a successful strategy for building a common life among churches. What we need, therefore, is another way of defining the church: one that recognizes how the most basic things are embodied in particular forms and how differences are indeed connected to what we have traditionally called essentials.

AN INCOMPLETE VIEW OF THE CHURCH

In the traditional definition of the church, we find a concentration on two central issues: the origin of the church in Jesus Christ and our common life in Christ. These issues are usually developed by means of images from the New Testament and the classic marks of the church. But note how little is said about the basic structures or systems that give life to a community over time. To be sure, there is often attention given to moments in the church's life such as fellowship, worship, and service (i.e., koinonia, liturgia, diaconia). But by and large, most of the things we would say about a social organization existing in time and space still need to be extracted from the words used to describe the origin of the church. While the deductions we make seem fairly obvious to us, we are not always as excited about the conclusions others draw from the foundational concepts. Just as disturbing is the fact that things left to be drawn out of a primary confession are inevitably given less attention or relegated to secondary status. Here I have in mind such issues as authority, relation to the world, expectations for the individual and the community, the enduring communal life of the church over time, ordination and the nature of ministry, the tension of sin and grace, different views of the sacraments, and the goal of history.

Given this tendency to omit so much of the church's life in the definition of the church, I am proposing that we take a more inclusive view. The problem is not that the traditional approach was too theological, so that the solution lies in switching to a sociological-historical analysis. Rather, the problem is that the traditional approach places all the emphasis on one aspect, namely, our relation to Christ. As a consequence, it either ignores other aspects of the church's life or relegates them to secondary status. Such an approach also generates a most serious problem: traditional claims about Jesus Christ are not made clear until we examine the relation of Jesus Christ to the other components of the church's life. Think again of the three Christians already mentioned (Roman Catholic, Lutheran, and Mennonite). They all affirm classic Christological affirmations from Nicea and Chalcedon, but these affirmations develop in each tradition in distinctive ways in light of the church's life and work. Who Jesus Christ is for each one is not fully comprehended simply by looking at the Nicene Creed. Lest this be misunderstood, the point is not that statements about Christ are too abstract or general, or that the only thing that matters is practical concerns. Instead, I am affirming that we need to think theologically about our union with Christ, *and* also think theologically about all of the things which determine the church's life and work as a community on earth. Only when we include into the theological discussion of the church all of these things shall we fully understand Jesus Christ as well as the so-called practical matters.

But what are these other components which need to be added? One is the way churches are defined by norms which govern faith and life. A second is the church as a community in space and time. Community is not something to be added as an after thought, reminding the reader that the believer united with Christ is also joined with others in Christ. Nor should it be described in such spiritual terms that one never thinks of a real community on earth. For these reasons it is important to speak of the community as one of the essential components of our definition of the church. It is a community with systems and practices that order and sustain the church's life (e.g., worship, music, education, leadership, service, and witness).

Three more components are inspired by Winthrop Hudson, the historian of American religion. In describing nineteenth-century divergent movements, Hudson lists three things a new movement requires. These may be summarized as: a principle of authority, a strategy for changing individuals and society, and a vision of the goal of history.[2] A new movement cannot exist over time without these three components. But these categories also ought to be used to understand the church itself, since they represent essential parts of a communal structure. In fact, if we think about the history of the church, we find that in every age these three issues

2. Hudson, *Religion in America*, 182.

were often either central to the creation of new forms of church life or were the cause of great division.

Gathering these together we find that our definition will be formed around six components, placed in this order: 1. origin; 2. norms; 3. authority; 4. a vision of history; 5. a theory of social change; 6. community life. At this point, these categories function in formal or generic terms. They constitute the outline used to describe the church as a community of Christ. In the following chapters we will see how they will embody value judgments giving the church its Christian character and leading to differentiation between churches.

Methodology

Thus far I have indicated the direction for the journey. Now a word about the methods used along the way. In the following pages I shall be talking about the church in three different ways: 1) a formal approach will provide the logical structure for defining the church; 2) a descriptive analysis will provide the material which makes up actual churches; 3) a constructive approach will allow us to make a case for a viable option for our time.

Starting With A Formal or Generic Definition

We begin by defining the church as a community of Christ in formal or generic terms. This gives us a logical structure in order to distinguish the church from other kinds of communities (e.g., social, political, or economic) and non-Christian religious communities. A formal definition is used when, for example, we define a chair in contrast from other pieces of furniture used for sitting. In one sense it is descriptive in answering the question: what makes a chair a chair? But to the extent that it explains the dynamics of a chair (i.e., what allows pieces of wood or metal to hold several hundred pounds so that we might make a chair), it moves from description to a higher level of understanding involving form and function. The formal definition offers an understanding of how and why the parts fit together. Once we understand the form of the church, we can then examine how particular churches embody this formal structure. But a word of caution is needed at this point: the formal analysis alone does not complete the definition of the church. It tells us something about the internal structure of churches, but is not a particular church in time and space.

It is tempting to test whether a formal definition is adequate. Could one define the church with more or less than these six components? Of course one could, by merging or expanding the categories. But the issue is not whether we could reduce or expand the list. Nor is it a true test to see if we could find some Christian community in the past twenty centuries that ignores one or more of these components. Rather, I think the validity of this approach should be measured by whether it helps us understand what holds churches together. Does it provide an inclusive framework for describing the variety of churches over twenty centuries? Will it allow us to do justice to the traditional affirmations about the church, as well as help us discern what motivates and divides churches in America today? Traditional discussions of the church that rely so heavily on Biblical imagery, the classic marks of the church, or the distinction between essentials and non-essentials tell us something very important about the church's origin and our union with Christ, but give less insight into why and how churches today are so deeply divided.

Many Forms of Faithfulness

If the formal definition provides a logical structure for thinking about the church, by contrast, the descriptive approach describes how actual churches embody the structural elements in specific ways. Here then we will attempt to describe the great variety of Christian traditions, treating it in two ways: First, to enumerate the range of actual churches, when for example, they embody different norms or principles of authority. Here we are interested in recognizing that Christians have been guided by the Spirit to form churches in many different ways. Therefore we need to acknowledge this variety. Second, to analyze strengths and weaknesses of historic options and evaluate them as resources for our situation. This analysis should shed light on why Christians differ and whether these differences can be resolved or transcended.

But why include a reminder of differences in a project that proposes to develop a viable definition of the church? The answer is that the essential components find expression in a great variety of symbols, structures, and practices. Not only do different churches define the essential components in different ways, even within one denomination or tradition the components of a healthy church display more than one option. It is, therefore, important to recognize such variety as many forms of faithfulness.

This approach stands in marked contrast to the attempt to define the true church in terms of the norms and components of one tradition. Such imperialism does violence to the complex pattern of traditions that represent alternate forms of Christianity. It is also a way of thinking which will not be tolerated by so many people in the church today, who have been formed by more than one tradition, or who find themselves in families where many traditions are present. Nor will such denominational absolutism stand the test of biblical and theological examination. I take it to be a special gift that the ecumenical theology of the past century has brought us to a place where we can see differences as many forms of faithfulness. We learn so much from one another when we listen to the affirmations others make. Not least of the wisdom gained is a clearer understanding of who we are. I have found that an important part of my journey in self-understanding is to see how my tradition is like and unlike other traditions. In a real sense I learn who I am by discovering who I am not. The good news is that I consider that there is a wide range of options on most topics. We are learning how to acknowledge the variety of Christian traditions while at the same time expressing preferences for certain theological ideas and church practices.

Reforming the Church: The Quest for a Viable Ecclesiology

If the second method enumerates specific forms of the church for the sake of appreciating and understanding the variety among Christians, the third method seeks to make a case for a specific form of the church. In this sense, it is prescriptive in the search for preferred options. This kind of discussion and debate is needed as we develop a view of the church. While the entire process begins with a formal outline for defining the church, and reviews the variety of actual traditions, it must finally conclude with a proposed ecclesiology for our time. My goal is to present to the reader the rich variety present in Christian traditions at each point along the way, while at the same time making a case for a specific theology of the church.

Can one do this without denying the value of variety or lapsing into the kind of dogmatism that insists that there is only one correct view? I admit that it is difficult, since there are notable examples of such practices among our ancestors. In honesty we must admit that we also find it easy to do this. But such dogmatism can be avoided if we bear several things in mind. First, acknowledging variety does not prevent one from making critical comments about strengths and weaknesses. The real test is whether one can speak openly of the weaknesses of one's own position. Second, we can affirm variety and still recognize that not all options are equally compelling or helpful in our situation. In some cases one may be led to conclude that serious mistakes were made. For example, it will be argued that adopting an apocalyptic vision that seeks to date the end of the world is not an appropriate way to understand the New Testament or understand what God is doing at this time. Finally and most important, in this essay my advocacy for a preferred option regarding the good news is just that, namely, a preferred option for ecumenical Christians in our time. I recognize other Christian traditions may not agree and prefer other ways for understanding the saving power of God in Christ. The whole burden of my study on atonement was to argue that there are many ways to understand Jesus Christ. If I appear to advocate something so strongly that it appears to violate the respect for one another which I affirm here, then such advocacy needs to be tempered by the unity we share in Christ.

Brief Outline of the Definition of the Church

We are now at a point where we may summarize in outline form the formal definition of the church. It consists of six components which describe the church not only with respect to its origin but its continued life as a community sustained over time. Since the six components are all essential to the church's life, one cannot prioritize them.

1. The church is a community whose identity and life originated in, and continue to be formed by, the new life of Jesus Christ and the Holy Spirit.

2. The church is a community which affirms norms for its faith and life.

3. The church is a community which claims authority.

4. The church is a community of hope with a vision of the future.

5. The church is a community which affirms power to transform individuals and society.

6. The church is a community which embodies in structures and practices the new life of Christ and the Spirit. These structures and practices include, but are not limited, to:

   - worship and spiritual life

   - music

   - proclamation within and outside the community

   - education at all stages of life and special efforts for leadership preparation

   - call and nurture of leaders

   - fellowship and care of one another

   - service and witness, in and outside the church

   - stewardship

   - physical presence in and against the world

   - ecumenical relations among Christians and other religious groups.

Two general comments are in order as we reflect on this outline. One has to do with the first component (Norms), which has not been discussed at length. To define the church one must make judgments about what is ultimately important. Finding a starting point, laying out the broad outline and making innumerable choices along the way—all these decisions require a guiding principle or norm. For example, does one begin by appealing to portions of the Bible, to the creeds or to formative events in the history of one's tradition? Such a question only opens the door to more questions and decisions: which portions of the Bible shall we use as the key to unlock all of the Scriptures? Shall membership in the community of Christ be determined by participation in churches claiming unbroken succession with St. Peter, or by affirmation of the true faith, or by a rebirth in the Spirit? The ease with which these questions can be posed emphasizes how every view of the church relies on normative judgments.

Recognizing the importance of norms is not, however, the hard part. The more difficult matter is how shall we select and define our norms.

Given the special challenge of our times, I think it is clear that certain approaches will not be helpful. We cannot begin by simply adopting denominational norms, as if everyone knows about or understands the great events and doctrines of one's tradition. Nor can one expect an immediate positive response by appealing to the Bible, assuming that such appeals trump all concerns. As noted above, we now have several generations of baptized and confirmed Christians who know little about the faith. What they do know is complicated by the ways our culture has misrepresented basic ideas, as well as their own bad experiences with churches. Indeed, many can name the day and the hour when the church spoke or acted in a repressive or exclusive way. Protestants seem to comprehend quite easily why practicing and non-practicing Roman Catholics do not trust the very symbols of authority, namely, the bishops. Years of repressive rule, the prohibitions against birth control, the exclusion of women from the priesthood, and of course, the abuse of children, have all eroded trust in the church's authority. But we seem to have great difficulty understanding why disaffected Protestants do not accept our appeals to the Bible and our normative documents. The fact is that we live in a world where all manner of repression and violence have been justified by appeals to the Bible. And if we have forgotten, we need to recall that among Christians who claim the primacy of Scripture, appeals to Scripture have seldom settled disagreements between these very Christians.

The conclusion to be drawn is not the exclusion of Scripture and tradition from the discussion, but a clearer awareness as to how they are used. We will need, at the outset, to make clear why Scripture and tradition have authority for the church. Moreover, we will also need to be prepared to explain how certain portions can be compelling, given the fact that listeners are repelled by other parts. For example, an appeal to Paul's great affirmation of salvation by grace may not be heard as good news by everyone because in other passages Paul appears to relegate women to secondary status or condone slavery. Some listeners cannot accept Paul as a guide for understanding Christian faith unless a way is found to neutralize some of Paul's destructive words. But this is but one example. A gathering of people may have multiple complaints about the Bible. We mistakenly assume that as long as we only appeal to certain passages that appear to be free from giving offense (e.g., God is love.) we can avoid the complaints. But the appeal to certain passages only highlights the problem: If certain passages are to be made authoritative, are all verses authoritative? If certain verses are to be ignored or rejected, what prevents us from rejecting all verses? I think people sense the urgency of these questions and want greater clarity on how we use Scripture. This further complicates the problem, since it is difficult to combine the long and hazardous discussion about our use of Scripture with a discussion of a specific issue. In the heat of a debate over homosexuality it is difficult to introduce for the first time that one does not accept every verse of the Bible.

It falls upon the preacher, teacher, or writer in this cultural situation to move quickly in establishing a case for norms. One cannot justify the authority of Scripture by appeals to some neutral reason or external objective standard. If such existed, it would be a virtual proof for the existence of God. I do not think such proofs exist. But we can provide a clear explanation why certain things have shown themselves to be trustworthy standards for the Christian life. This can also be done with the recognition that many readers will need more than the standard code language of the beloved community. The key to explaining why Scripture, creed or tradition may serve as norms is to point to what they witness, namely, the saving power of God in Jesus Christ. Things are turned upside down when we seek the source of authority in these texts or traditions themselves. This has unfortunately led churches to try to create on earth absolute fortresses of an infallible Bible or infallible doctrine, only to be confounded by the limits of such claims. A theology of the church is not a place to hide the limits and sins of the church, but to confess that even the church still lives in the tensions between sin and grace.

A second comment has to do with the order of the components. While the order does not represent an order of importance, nevertheless it can be construed that way. Whatever is listed in last place too easily is considered an add-on, diminished in importance by the mere fact that so much is said before we even get to it. I choose to place the discussion of the community's life at the end—not because it is least important—but because it gathers into itself all that has been said before. Moreover, the present life of the community is affected by the way we understand the origin of the church, norms, authority, our vision of the future, and the means of social change. To speak of the church's communal life in Christ before these topics are discussed implies that such life is unaffected by the preceding issues. It is as if the vision of the future—which is so often placed as a last thing in spite of the irony of such placement—is an after-thought. Or, to use an example from the Mennonites, it would be to suggest that life together in Christ is not affected by the Anabaptist relation to the world or their principle of authority.

Concluding Comments

Thus far I have outlined the way this analysis of the church shall proceed. The advantage of the traditional approach is that it restricts the discussion to a fairly limited field of inquiry, with the expectation that the matters discussed will be considered essentials shared by all Christians. But this overlooks the fact that while most Christians may affirm these essentials, they do so in quite different ways. It ignores the ways these so-called essentials are linked to many other aspects of the church's life. This severely limits the discussion of the church, especially since these so-called non-essential aspects are crucial in differentiating churches from one another. This study assumes that we cannot reform the church unless we see how faith, structure and practice are connected.

The approach offered here, however, does face a major challenge. If we are to define the church in terms of the six components, and also acknowledge the variety of Christian traditions, we must ask: How can the very things which have caused so much division and conflict be included in the definition of the church? This is a serious issue and could be avoided in one of the following ways: 1) We could define the church from the perspective of only one tradition. 2) We could try once more to define the church by a small set of theological affirmations, which all Christians may seem to share—or ought to share. The first approach represents a retreat into a denominational enclave, which simply cannot be justified. The second approach again raises the question whether the traditional approach is the answer, since it appears to solve the problem. Against the second option the following must be stated:

First, if we choose to speak only of a short list of so-called core convictions, in the hope of finding a kind of higher common ground, then we exclude from discussion so much of the faith and practice of the church. The church is not fully described by the image Body of Christ, or the Protestant shorthand of Word and sacraments. It has its origin in Word and sacraments, but it is more than these. The church has a complex life as a social organization enduring over time. It includes elements relating to authority, the strategies for changing people and society, ways churches interact with the world, and a vision of the goal of history. The communal life exists only when sustained by worship, music, education, fellowship, witness, and service. These must be included in our definition of the church because communities consider them essential. Put in another way, the distinction between essentials and non-essentials does not reflect how traditions view their faith and life. The so-called essentials are not generic universals but become, in the faith and life of traditions, quite specific. The things which are so easily ruled non-essentials become invested with value because they embody in known and unknown ways the primary norms of the community. For example, mainline Protestants and Mennonites do not have exactly the same view of Christ, but differ on just war theory. Rather, each group, thinks about Christ in a specific way, which leads them to their divergent theories of peace making. The practical policies regarding the state and violent coercion are not addendum.

Second, it is necessary to include the contentious issues in our definition of the church because these are the things that separate us and cause us great difficulty within and between traditions. In effect, I am proposing that we actually admit that Christians are deeply divided over issues which they do not deem non-essential. I would even go further: I think all parties will find some comfort in being told that the essential elements of the church do in fact have great variety. The differences may come into the church—not as inferior parts, as things to be held in shame—but as ways we perceive the new life in Christ as both gift and promise.

This means that this study of the church shall be carried out in the midst of the tension between defining the church in a way which is inclusive of all Christians and which recognizes the range of differences between the traditions. From my perspective, this does not mean that we are invited into a wild and disharmonious shouting match of conflicting ideas. If we affirm that the church is the community of new life in Christ and the Spirit, all parties must accept that Christ is Lord of the Church. This means that the church, with its complex life as a social community in time and space, consists of many forms and varieties. Christians differ on small and big issues; they interpret and embody the so-called core essentials in different ways. But Christ is still Lord of all and unites all in his

Body and at his table. At Christ's table no one may claim that he or she alone is Christian.

Here it is helpful to speak of our unity in Christ in terms of the famous imagery of 1 Corinthians 12. In this passage Paul speaks of the variety of spiritual gifts among members and proposes that they are all helpful for the common life, just as the various parts of the body are united in one living person. Most important, he affirms that the head of the church, holding all of the parts together, is Jesus Christ. Now Protestants tend to link 1 Corinthians 12 with the affirmation of catholicity, namely, that the church catholic includes many different parts. This obviously allows Protestants to deal with their many divisions and to argue that the whole church is not represented unless all the parts are put together like a 2000-piece puzzle. The argument concludes with the affirmation that each part brings a special gift. But I want to use 1 Corinthians 12 to interpret our unity in Christ, not to justify our variety. Paul is saying that we are united even though we—the individual parts—are very different in form and function. No one may claim he or she does not need another, or is superior to the other. Rather, the most striking differences in form and function are united. Where did we get the idea that variety or difference only relates to non-essentials? I think the early church was quite aware that Christians throughout the Mediterranean differed on just about everything except the new life in Christ—but even that was described in different ways in the New Testament. Christ unites all of the different parts and all are essentials.

The fact is that we differ. This is not news. What is good news is that we who are so different are united in Christ. Some may feel it only makes things worse to admit variety and difference in the definition of the church. But that, I think, assumes that we can be united only if we conceal our differences. Paul declares that we are united in spite of our differences. In this sense it helps to include reference to them in our discussion of the church: first it forces each side to explain how their understanding of the essentials reveals the new life in Christ; second, it forces us to remember that our debating, and shouting, are done in the presence of the One who unites us when our faith and practices are so diverse.

One last introductory comment. As we work our way through the discussion of the church's life, we will draw connections between essential affirmations and the church's mission, rather than waiting to discuss mission in a final chapter. By speaking of mission in this way, we will avoid the error of thinking that the church can have its life without mission. In fact, they are inseparable. The church does not first have its existence and then adds on a mission. Nor does the church need to go searching for a mission, or hold a conference to determine what its mission can or should be. The mission of the church is rooted in its very being and naturally flows from the new life in Christ. If the mission is not clear, go back to the basic affirmations about the church's life. Every essential affirmation about the church contains a mandate for mission and points to a need in the members as well as the world. For example, if the church is born of grace, then the church must find its mission in being gracious to those in need, or quite specifically, those who live in disgrace.

one

The Origin of the Church

The First Essential Component:

The church is a community whose identity and life originated in, and continue to be formed by, the new life of Jesus Christ and the Holy Spirit.

THE CHURCH IS BOUND to its origin. From an historical perspective, it comes to be in and through the events connected with Jesus Christ. But these events are not merely the occasion for something which comes later. Now as well as then, the origin forms the identity and life of the church. The reason is that the church was created, and continues to exist, by the life flowing from the crucified and risen Jesus. There is no getting around or beyond Jesus. Past, present, and future merge. The church remembers past events but celebrates the presence of Christ and the Spirit. It looks to a future defined by Christ.

The starting point, then, is that the church was and is formed by the events of Jesus Christ. But what is the nature of that community-forming process? How did the process shape the identity and life of believers? Just when one thinks one has found an answer to that question, one is faced with another: Why did communities confessing Christ develop in so many different ways in faith and practice? That is, why was not the formative process uniform? That churches are dependent on Jesus Christ is fairly easy to establish. But the other issues are quite complex and defy a simple answer. What is needed in this first chapter is to identify the creative factors instrumental in forming the community as well as producing diversity among communities. We will be looking for the way events form believers and the community they come to share. Such events have creative power in forming persons, in generating multiple options as well as setting limits. For example, grace appears to be a major factor, but it takes many forms in speaking to different people, and it clearly rules out many things. Once these factors have been set before us we can then, in following chapters, describe how they interact and finally move to a general theory regarding the formation of specific churches.

The Birth of the Church

Let us begin by re-setting the birthday of the church. If the church comes into being by events connected with Jesus, then the birth of the church is not Pentecost (when the Spirit was bestowed upon the followers of Jesus fifty days after Easter). Rather, it is the coming of Jesus, his baptism and receiving the Spirit, and his proclamation of the coming of the Kingdom of God. The church has its birth in the moment women and men responded to Jesus' call to follow. To be sure, these people must go through trials and changes, but what happens at Pentecost is a continuation of the community gathered by Jesus. This judgment about the birth of the church also prompts the further conclusion: Jesus intended to create on earth a gathering of people faithful to God and formed by a new covenant. To explain and support this perspective, let us consider two themes: a) the primacy of God's act; b) the intervention of holiness.

The Primacy of God's Act

The early church speaks of the origin of the church as a creation of God. For example, the disciples are never described as founders of the church, but as people who are *called* by God (ecclesia) and people who are *sent* by Christ (apostles). The passive voice makes clear their self-definition as members of this new community. From this it follows that the existence of the church is forever tied to the story of Jesus—his life, death, and resurrection—and the gift of Christ's Spirit at Pentecost. Every aspect of the church's life is dependent upon God's saving power. Such dependence must be given expression by affirming the primacy of God's wisdom re-vealed in Christ as well as the living relation of the church to Christ: the church has no life other than that which it receives in Christ and in the Spirit. In short: God did it.

The primacy of God's act becomes apparent if we look at the way the Gospels are laid out. It has been suggested that the Gospels are long in-troductions to the narrative of the last week (Palm Sunday to Easter). The only problem with this suggestion is that it could minimize the impor-tance of Jesus' life—an approach to be avoided. We could not understand the last week without the narratives of Jesus' actions, sayings, parables, wonders, and the way he related to the people portrayed in the Gospels. But the point of the suggestion is worth considering: the story of Jesus culminates in his faithfulness to God in the face of betrayal, suffering and death, and God's intervention in raising him to be Lord. What the early Christians were confronted with, therefore, is that everything turns on his crucifixion and resurrection. Once convinced that he was vindicated by God and made Lord, then everything had to be re-evaluated: what he said and did, what they said and did in response to him, and what God was doing in the entire process. For the early church, the astonishing fact was that the crucified had been made Lord. That strange, terrifying, and wonder-filled statement meant that new life was now presented to them, but it could never be disconnected from the one who was rejected and crucified.

This brings us to a most difficult and threatening aspect of the story. The Gospels do more than give God the glory. They deliberately portray most of the characters in the story as misunderstanding, resisting, or be-traying Jesus. There is a profound sense that God's action to redeem the world happens in spite of and against the resistance of human thought and action. Consider a few examples:

- In Mark, when Jesus performs signs and wonders, the onlookers are astonished but do not understand.

- James and John ask Jesus for permission to seize power and rule when the Kingdom comes.

- In the transfiguration, James and John want to stay on the mountain, but Jesus insists that they must come down to continue his mission.

- When Jesus declares that the Son of Man must suffer, Peter rebukes Jesus.

- When Jesus is betrayed by one disciple and arrested, Peter denies that he knows Jesus.

- In John's gospel, Nicodemus, a teacher of religion, does not understand that one must be reborn of the Spirit. The Samaritan woman at the well cannot comprehend how Jesus can provide living water when he does not have a jar. The disciples cannot understand how Jesus can provide the bread of life since he has not been to the village market.

- Beyond the Gospels, we find that Paul, the great missionary to the Gentiles, starts out persecuting the Christians until he meets Christ on the road to Damascus. How amazing that one who claimed wisdom is struck blind and receives new sight in the light of Christ.

- Peter, the leader of the disciples, is slow to comprehend that Jesus Christ means the inclusion of Gentiles.

- Finally, in spite of the fact that men dominated the leadership of the early church, what are we to make of the fact that the first witnesses to the resurrected Christ were women? Not Peter, James or John, not the remaining disciples, but the faithful women. One does not need much imagination to see in this text the fulfillment of Jesus' own words that the last shall be first and the first last.

When we view all these incidents one must conclude that there is a self-critical perspective at work in the gospels as well as the letters of the New Testament. Though Jesus is baptized, anointed with the Spirit, and tempted, he sets his face toward Jerusalem and nothing will prevent him from proclaiming the coming of God's rule. Not the ineptitude and betrayal of his own disciples, not the opposition of religious leaders, nor the conspiracies of Roman leaders.

Perhaps the most dramatic affirmation of the primacy of God's initiative is in the birth narratives. These narratives only appear in the Gospels of Matthew and Luke; the other two writers (Mark and John) find other ways to begin their gospels. Whatever historical value we give to these narratives, we need to ask what Matthew and Luke intended by beginning with this material. Each, in his own way, affirms that God is doing a surprising and also terrifying work. Nearly everyone is troubled or afraid: Zechariah and Elizabeth (the parents of John the Baptist), Mary and Joseph, and finally the shepherds. The angels are repeatedly telling them not to be afraid! Notice the different reactions people have to the announced events: Zechariah cannot believe the angel, and is struck speechless, whereas Mary trusts the angel and is called "Blessed" by Elizabeth. Herod, fearing for his throne, conspires with the wise men and then slaughters the innocent male children. By contrast, the prayers and prophecies of Zechariah, Elizabeth, Mary, and Simeon are filled with affirmations of saving power. God will lift up the poor and overthrow the proud and mighty. Now before their very eyes the promises of forgiveness and peace will be fulfilled. God's anointed now appears in their midst to redeem God's people and fulfill the promises to Abraham and the House of Israel. All this, however, will not happen without fear, strife, division, and even death. In virtually every sequence, Matthew and Luke give us signals of what is to happen later in the story. If you read the birth narratives carefully, the final week is not a surprise at all.

One aspect of the account in Luke has always caught my attention. This is the exchange between Elizabeth and Mary. Recall that both Elizabeth and her husband are old, considered past the time of childbearing. Elizabeth lives with the traditional burden of reproach for not having children. Thus the announcement that she will have a son is good news, though it was quite unbelievable for her husband, Zechariah. When Elizabeth greets Mary, Elizabeth pronounces a blessing upon this woman who believes the Lord's promise. Then Mary sings the famous song now known as the Magnificat: "My soul magnifies the Lord. . . ." This brings us to the crucial question. The opening lines of the Magnificat come from a song sung by Hannah in the Old Testament. Hannah thanks God for giving her a child in her old age. This child will be the prophet Samuel, who anoints King David. But why does Luke have Mary sing this song? Mary is young and not even married. It would be more appropriate for Elizabeth to sing this song, since her situation resembles that of Hannah. The answer lies in the birth narratives of the patriarchs of Israel. If we read the story of Abraham and Sarah, we find that Sarah is barren and is given a child to fulfill the promise of the covenant. Both Abraham and Sarah doubted that God would ever fulfill the promise. A less dramatic version occurs with their son Isaac and his wife Rebekah. Isaac prays to God for a child and the birth of Jacob and Esau is seen as another instance of God's faithfulness. Here then is the answer to our question: the Magnificat connects Mary to Hannah, who stands in a tradition of women who bear children only by the gracious intervention of God. Luke has Mary sing Hannah's song because Luke wishes to place Mary and her son Jesus in the tradition of other great leaders in Israel: they are born against human doubt and despair, given as signs of God's surprising grace and faithfulness.

What then may we conclude from the way the Gospels describe Jesus' birth and his followers? Is it not to make clear that whatever happened is the work of God, rather than something of human design, power or invention? And what is this work of God? Is it not an amazing outpouring of grace and power to restore human life, to lift up the fallen and forsaken? If this interpretation is correct, then the affirmation of the primacy of God's action relates directly to the formation of the church's self-understanding. To say God is the giver of life is to say we have received a gift. Here then we face the defining moment for the church's identity and being: *The church has its life only as a life given by a gracious God.* For this reason Paul must coin new language when he declares that we live *in Christ*. The church has no existence except that given to it in the new life of Jesus Christ. For the church or its members to declare ownership of the church, or to try to control it, is to deny the true life in Christ.

Having established this central point, it is appropriate to enumerate briefly several consequences that flow from this affirmation for the church's life and mission.

1. If the church's life is given to it by the action of God in Jesus Christ and the Spirit, then the church will be a community of joyful remembrance and gratitude for what God has done and is doing in the world. It is in this moment of remembrance that *confession of faith, education,* and *evangelism* arise, i.e., telling the story for ourselves and our children, for those seeking good news, and for a witness to the world.

2. There is another kind of remembrance which keeps the church close to its origin: this is the *honest admission of our resistance* to what God has done and our unwillingness to accept the gift or the promise. At a later point we will need to discuss how the church's confession of sin forms a part of the church's total life. Some find

this topic troublesome, burdened with talk of guilt and judgment. There may well have been times when the remembrance of sin overshadowed the joy of new life. But avoiding such extremes cannot justify the failure to remember that it is God who has redeemed us from our self-centeredness and idolatry. On this matter the Book of Deuteronomy offers witness: true faith is to remember that we did not create the world and all the things that sustain us, but that we are the recipients of the things that make for life. For Deuteronomy, the opposite of faith is not disbelief but forgetting. If we forget who has made us and what we have received, then we deceive ourselves and are tempted by pride and self-righteousness. In a similar way, the church must resist the construction of a false self-understanding by confessing what God has done and remember that we resist being marked by God's gift.

3. If the church lives by this twofold remembrance, then it will be a *community of praise and thanksgiving*, giving God the glory. The worship of God is therefore directly rooted in the church's origin as a gifted people who have received grace upon grace. This leads to the further conclusion: the first mission of the church is to be a community of remembrance and worship. This means that mission is not something totally outside the church gathered. To the contrary, it is part of the mission of the church to be a community of joyful celebration, to create harmonious music amid the noise of the world, and to be a confessing community in an idolatrous world.

The Intervention of Holiness

God's act of grace always moves toward new life. The Scriptures which Jesus relies upon declare that God is love and holy. This means that God's love, which surely includes an embrace of acceptance, also wills to create and restore life. In English the root word for *holy* produces a strikingly suggestive cluster of words: holy, heal, one, and health are all derived from the same stem. The moral standard of holiness is tied to the goal of healing, justice aims at reuniting the estranged, judgment dreams of a new time of health in God's commonwealth. This suggests that when holiness enters the world as a gift, it always contains a promise of new life.

But just as the gift encounters our resistance, so the intervention of holiness stands against sin, the powers of evil and death itself. God's action interrupts what we consider to be the normal state of things in this world: selfishness, the use and abuse of all things and people, dishonesty and betrayal, the horrors of war and genocide, disease, and death. Like the cast of characters in the gospels, we know how easy it is to settle into such a world. On this point Paul speaks with great force: we find ourselves held in bondage to the powers of this world. Not only do they disrupt and violate life, they come to dominate life by the fear they generate and the time and effort devoted to avoiding them. The good news for Paul and the early Christians is that what happened in Christ and the Spirit is the intervention of new life. This means a liberation, a freeing from the powers, and especially the fear that dominates us. It also means a healing, a re-creation, or empowerment.

The Presence of New Life

What is the nature of this new reality which originates in God's intervention? To find the answer we need to avoid taking the wrong path. The church does not originate in new teaching or ideas, now available for all to read. Even when these ideas are given theological form and blessed by churches as official doctrine, we still have not located the new reality. Nor is it found in ethical commands or a set of values. The claim that Jesus' moral teachings are distinct and/or set apart from other religious teachings does not bring us to the church's life. It certainly leads us astray to suggest that Christianity is a set of liberating ideas that we can claim as our own and find the will to practice in the face of a cold and violent world.

Against these well known reductions of Christian faith to ideas and values, we find an entirely different description of the church's origin in its early confessions. To be sure, there is great variety in the parts of the New Testament. The research over the last two centuries has emphasized the contrasts and differences between these writings. This has produced a wealth of information and reflection on the uniqueness of each part, but great caution regarding the unity of the books. Time and again we are advised that each of the Gospels and Paul provide very different images and themes to describe Jesus Christ. But for our purposes we need to see the ways these writings converge regarding the birth and life of the church.

Paul's writings (which predate the Gospels) overflow with a sense of excitement generated by the new reality of Christ the risen Lord. His focus is on the way cross and resurrection represent God's judgment and plan for salvation. Sin, death, and the powers of this world, along with human claims to righteousness and spiritual power, are set against God's grace in Christ. A new creation has dawned, marked by freedom from the powers of this world and reconciliation with God and one another. If the world was held in bondage, so now in Christ we are free to become sons and daughters of God and heirs of God (Rom 8:12–25). If we once saw all things from a human point of view—or assumed nothing could change— now we are given a new creation. The old self has died and a new self has been born (1 Cor 5:16–21). Lest we think Paul is engaging in speculation, recall his description of his conversion: confronted by the risen Christ he was struck blind, gave up his old life, and received new sight in the light of Christ. How fitting that he should later describe all Christians as children of light! In all of this Paul makes it clear that the new life results only from the intervention of God's grace. Moreover, Paul can only describe the new spiritual life by coining new images: we live *in Christ* or *in the Spirit*. The new being finds expression in the image of the *Body of Christ*: Christ is head of the church and we are the members, with different forms and functions, joined together. We no longer live by ourselves or for ourselves, but our lives are open to God and find a new center in God's will in Christ. In this new creation, the old distinctions of male and female, slave and free, and even Jew and Gentile are replaced by a common life in Christ.

The Gospel of John also affirms God's initiative in uniting all things in Christ. Jesus is the Word made flesh, who is the way to the true knowledge of God. There is an unfolding love of God from the Father to the Son to the disciples and finally to the world, so that all might know God and live in love. But the new life is hidden from those who cannot see beyond worldly things: a teacher cannot understand that one must be born again; a Samaritan woman does not see how Jesus can give her living water; the disciples do not comprehend how Jesus is the bread of life. John's Gospel repeatedly reveals that Jesus brings new life which the world does not see. When John describes this new life, it is quite clear that believers are joined to Jesus in a spiritual union. They are dependent upon Jesus and receive from him the new life. Consider the great image of the vine and branches, which is but one of the many organic images John uses to describe how the Christian community has life only in relation to the risen Lord.

While it is clear that Paul and John use very different approaches and images, they agree on two major points regarding new life in Christ. First, in both cases the new life is based on the priority of God's action in Christ, which is clearly an intervention of holiness in this world. Second, the message of salvation is the invitation to participate in a new way of being in this world. If Paul seeks to root out all claims to self-righteousness in proclaiming justification by grace and the mission to the Gentiles, John speaks of being reborn into unity with Christ in the unfolding love of God. The similarities of the two dominant images of Body of Christ and Vine and Branches are also striking: both affirm a spiritual union between members and Christ as well as between the members themselves; both affirm a dependency of members upon Christ the Lord. Whereas Paul's image allows him to affirm the unity of members who have different gifts, John's image makes clear that actualizing the gifts of the new life depends upon our connection with Christ.

The differences between the Synoptic Gospels (Matthew, Mark, and Luke) and these themes in Paul and John are well known. Many of the powerful images and themes in Paul and John do not appear in the Synoptics. But too often the Synoptics are separated from Paul and John by a process of selective reading. For example, if we only focus on Jesus' teachings of love, with the parables as illustrations, then these three Gospels would indeed stand apart from Paul and John. Herein lies our problem. This view has more to do with the way we choose to read the Synoptics than with what they actually say. Such a reading requires that we ignore the beginning and ending of each of these gospels, which announce that God is doing something for the salvation of the world. Baptized and anointed by the Spirit, Jesus will proclaim the coming of the Kingdom of God in the face of the powers of Satan and the opposition of worldly rulers. But where, you ask, does the idea of participation in Christ appear in the teachings and actions of Jesus in Matthew, Mark, and Luke? We are obviously not going to find the distinctive images of Paul and John. What we do find is that Jesus' teachings and actions are set in the context of the Kingdom of God, now breaking into this world. All of the commands make no sense outside of Jesus' pronouncement that the Kingdom of God has come and

we live in a new time. Jesus never suggests the command to love is directed toward autonomous, self-made persons. Rather it comes to those who
no longer serve two masters, who are willing to lose their lives for Jesus'
sake and the gospel's, and who are willing to follow him. Furthermore,
these sayings and commandments were remembered in the context of the
community of new life in Christ, the risen Lord. Only because our lives
are gifted by grace and freed from the powers of this world is it possible
to risk loving one another—let alone speak of love. This is quite clear in
Matthew's account of the great commission: the command to baptize and
teach is preceded by the presence of Jesus and followed by his promise to
be with us to the end of the world. Matthew, Mark, and Luke are not prior
to the church and its bold faith in Christ, but stand with Paul and John in
churches proclaiming new life in Christ.

What are the consequences for the life of the church if it exists only
as a new creation in Christ?

- If the church is a new creation—a new way of being in the world—
  then it has been *set apart from the world*. The Rule of God and the
  new life in Christ are different from life lived for ourselves amid the
  warfare of this world. How this sense of being set apart relates to life
  in this world is a great challenge facing the church. But the distinctive character of the new life in Christ will be lost if we do not begin
  with the fact that it is set apart.

- If the church lives in the new creation, then it receives the *freedom
  from the powers of this world and the freedom to be sons and daughters
  of God*. The twofold character of this freedom has always been a part
  of the church's being: to be liberated from sin, guilt, the fear of death,
  and the endless warfare of this world; to live for God and neighbor, knowing that one's identity and worth are gifts of God. Luther
  declared this boldly in his treatise on Christian freedom; in our
  time Gustavo Gutierrez rightly described our freedom in personal,
  religious and social-political terms.[1] Such freedom is grounded in
  God's gift and promise. It determines both the life and mission of
  the church.

---

1. Cf. Luther, "The Freedom of a Christian," 42–85; Gutierrez, *A Theology of Liberation*, 102–3.

- If the church's self-understanding is grounded in the gift and promise of new life, then it will always be *a community of hope.* Too often this hope has either been lost or simply transferred to rewards in heaven. But Christians hope for the fulfillment of the promise given in Christ for the redemption of the world. This includes the hope of resurrection but also the transformation of our lives and the earth into God's peaceable kingdom.

A Critical Question

Now we need to pause and ask a critical question: why should this description of the view of the early church matter to us? In the Introduction the reader was assured that arguments would not be settled simply by appealing to Scripture or tradition. So, why cannot we affirm that the church is something we create, such as a social contract of the faithful? And why cannot we live as Christians on the basis of our ability to respond to the call of Christ? Much of contemporary American religion is based on these assumptions. So what is wrong with them? The short answer is that they don't work—either very well or at all. The long answer involves appealing to the individual and collective experience of Christians.

First, whenever churches forget that they are God's creation and dependent upon Christ, they become dependent upon something else. This usually takes the form of depending on culture. Whether it is a state church or, as in America, an unofficial religion of the status quo, the church soon mirrors the cultural values and sees its role as providing divine sanction for the society. How strange that we object to this in other nations but find it acceptable in America.

Second, the modern age has overflowed with optimism regarding the human condition, in philosophy, economics, political, and social theories. But time and again these theories, relying upon claims to innocence or the perfectibility of human life, have failed with disastrous consequences. Even the reform movements, intended to correct the problems, seem to run out of energy over time. Unable to keep alive the original vision, they fail to interpret either their successes or failures in terms of sin and grace. But in a shocking way, the sad history of the past two centuries does not seem to diminish this confidence in self-reliance. For example, no matter how many times self-regulation has proven to be an illusion in Wall Street or mining and oil drilling, many still insist that it is the answer.

Third, consider the gradual shifts over several generations with respect to active participation in religious communities. It is not hard to track the movement from active membership to non-practicing to total separation from the tradition. Good people with the best of intentions find themselves in a predicament: since they do not know or practice the tradition, they are unable to nurture their children in the faith. When one ceases to remember how the church was born and how it is dependent on the grace of God, the substance of the Christian life is gone. Faced with such a situation, parents and children are tempted to fall back on some form of self-reliance or some authoritarian program that promises to fill the void. Consider the strategies for self-help in popular religion in America. Here we find the almost endless optimism of Americans channeled to solving all manner of personal problems. These strategies tend to exaggerate our powers for reform. This is partly due to our optimism, but also due to our insistence on denying the tragic side of our personal or social history. As a result we become candidates for the inward quest for true light, or the message of self-empowerment from the Crystal Cathedral in the hope that a bit of meaning will be added on to our lives. But these approaches are notorious for ignoring the great moral disasters of our time. I do not find much evidence for our ability to reform ourselves without falling into the very self-centeredness that was the cause of our problem in the first place.

The long answer then is that the early church's views are proposed for us for two reasons: 1) they offer a more realistic view of the human condition in the face of the brokenness and great catastrophes of our time; 2) they point to the hope of new life in Christ. They are words of hope because they are not dependent on our ideas and energy, but speak of God's gracious intervention into our lives. The church lives in the realization that what is needed is not another try using variations on human powers, but a willingness to receive the gift and promise of Christ.

Images of New Life

Churches celebrate and understand the new life in Jesus Christ in different ways. The great variety and richness of these interpretations tell us several things. On the one hand, they indicate that in every place and time the story of Jesus was essential for the church's faith and life. Nowhere was it possible to ignore, set aside or minimize Jesus' life, death, and resurrection. On the other hand, the interpretations of Jesus increased in number because communities sought to proclaim the good news in ways appropriate for their time and place. Every interpretation relies on a powerful image that connects God's saving power with a particular human need. When the images are able to support a comprehensive interpretation of how Jesus reveals new life, they expand to what we now call theories of atonement. But it is best to keep in mind the original image, which offered creative insight for understanding the cross.

For most of the twentieth century, the great variety of images was overlooked. This was primarily due to the influence of Gustaf Aulen's book, *Christus Victor*.[2] Aulen argued that there are three theories of atonement: a transactional view (often referred to as penal substitution), a moral influence theory, and finally a view of conquest over Satan, which Aulen called *Christus Victor*. The transactional view was identified with the Roman Catholic interpretation of the Mass as a sacrifice offered to God. As such it portrayed Jesus' death as satisfaction for the penalty laid upon sinners by a just God. Aulen rejected this because it made Jesus' death appear to be a work offered to God, rather than God's action toward us. In the process Aulen also identified this view with St. Anselm. We should note that the theory of penal substitution also appears among orthodox Protestants and is boldly defended by the nineteenth-century Presbyterian Charles Hodge. For many conservative Protestants it is a required article of faith. The second view was tied to Abelard and quickly dismissed by Aulen, on the grounds that it reduced the cross to the liberal message of love. Having eliminated two views, we are therefore left with only one valid theory, namely the interpretation which sees Christ conquering Satan, thereby liberating the world from sin, death, and demonic powers. If one reads Aulen in terms of his theological context, one can see how he positions Protestant theology (i.e., Lutheran) in between Roman Catholics and liberal Protestants. Each of these, according to Aulen, misconstrues saving power. The one reduces it to a transaction offered to an angry God, the other eliminates the importance of the cross and resurrec-

---

2. Cf. Aulen, *Christus Victor: An Historical Study of the Three Main Types of the Idea of the Atonement*.

tion by translating these events into the message of eternal love. But in the process Aulen misinterprets both Anselm and Abelard so badly that they are discarded from serious consideration. Far more serious is the fact that when all is said and done, we are left with but one theory of saving power.

To begin a process of thinking about atonement in a new way, *Saving Power: Theories of Atonement and Views of the Church* sought to free us from the stranglehold Aulen had placed on this subject.[3] The first step was to offer an alternative interpretation of Anselm, and then in turn, Abelard. Once these two theologians were rescued from the theological scrap heap, the way was open to suggest that there are many images of saving power. What followed was an analysis of ten different images. This was possible once one recognizes that each image speaks of a specific form of saving power in relation to a specific human need. Since they speak to different issues, they need not conflict with one another but actually point to the fullness of God's grace. In this sense it is inappropriate to ask which theory is the right one, since each points to some aspect of saving power that Christians wish to affirm. The one exception to this is the theory of penal substitution. This theory is seriously flawed since it makes God a passive object of action offered by Jesus Christ, thereby allowing his death to be seen as having significance in and of itself. This criticism has existed for centuries and has been revived in our time, especially by feminist writers. I included this theory in the study because it is affirmed by so many traditions. I believe it can be a valid interpretation only if it is reworked to make it consistent with the fundamental themes of the New Testament.

These theories are summarized here for several reasons: First, before we can draw any conclusions about the way Jesus affects the formation of the church, we need to examine the way Christians have remembered and celebrated the new life he brings. The fact is that Christians do this is many ways. While each tradition may gravitate toward one or more images of saving power, nothing prevents churches from utilizing more than one image. In fact, the liturgy, preaching, and hymns tend to follow Scripture in embracing many images of saving power without concern for consistency or how they relate.

---

3. The summary of the ten interpretations in this chapter does not include the extensive footnotes and technical comments contained in the earlier work. To examine these, cf. Schmiechen, *Saving Power: Theories of Atonement and Forms of the Church*.

Second, once we have a sense of the many images of Jesus, we can then begin to examine the way specific churches are formed. This, however, is a complex process, which can not be fully understood until we reach the final chapters. But at this point it may be said that images of Jesus are one of the contributing factors in the formation of churches, shaping preaching, the sacraments and personal spiritual life. In some cases, one image dominates a specific tradition. An example would be the way Roman Catholic art, sculpture, and symbols focus on the *sacrifice* of Jesus. From the high altar to side chapels and the Stations of the Cross, the faithful are invited to consider and adore the faithfulness of Jesus. This does imply that such practice follows the theology of penal substitution. But as we shall see, there are other sources for using the image of sacrifice to interpret Jesus.

The ten images are briefly summarized here, organized into four broad groups dealing with forgiveness, liberation, the purposes of God, and reconciliation.

Forgiveness

1. The image of *sacrifice* has a rich background, drawing upon two sources. One uses the symbolism of Jewish ritual for purification of sinners, which is different from offerings of thanksgiving. Here sacrifice was not offered to appease God, but instituted by God to reunite sinners with God. Two ideas from Jewish sacrifice play prominent roles in Christian liturgy and theology: that the sacrifice of Jesus *covers* (i.e., contains and/or neutralizes) the power of sin and that Jesus *takes away* the sins of the world. The second source for the use of sacrifice is general human experience: someone gives time, talent or life itself for us. Most Americans, unfamiliar with first-century Jewish rituals or the New Testament, will respond to the image of sacrifice in terms of their general experience. But both uses of sacrifice appear in art, liturgies, sermons, and hymns.

2. Paul uses the image of *justification by grace* to interpret Jesus' death and resurrection. The image is drawn from legal practice, only it contains a surprise. Imagine having broken the law and knowing that one is guilty. One therefore stands without any justification or claim of righteousness. This follows the simple logic of what we take to be moral order: one should get what one deserves, i.e., if you sin, you

will be punished; if you do good things, you will be rewarded. But Paul does not see this happening in the story of Jesus. Not only does an innocent person die on the cross, but God does not use this as reason to punish the world. In fact, God raises the crucified to be Lord and thereby invites the world into a new covenant. This surprise ending requires an alteration in language: now we are justified or made right before God in spite of our sin, not on the basis of our actions, but solely by the grace of God.

3. Another legal image dominates the faith and practice of many Roman Catholics and Protestants. This is the idea of *penal substitution*. It draws upon one of the earliest confessions about Jesus: that Jesus died for me. In itself this phrase can have many positive meanings. But in this case, it is combined with the legal image of an innocent person taking the place of the guilty, receiving their punishment, and thereby freeing the guilty from the obligation of punishment. This presupposes the idea of justice as a balance of payments, which requires punishment. Thus Jesus substitutes himself for us guilty sinners in payment to God's justice. Problems abound with this view: it is hard to find in the New Testament the idea that Jesus dies to satisfy the demands of justice. Many object to making the death of Jesus an end in itself, since it appears to sanction violence as the means of salvation. Some Protestants, especially Pietists and Anabaptists, affirm penal substitution in a much softer way, namely, that Jesus died for us sinners to show God's love. For them, less attention is given to the demand to satisfy justice or the graphic images of blood and suffering.

Liberation

4. Jesus has also been interpreted as God's *liberation* of people from sin, death, and the powers of this world. This does not replace forgiveness, but affirms that we suffer from more than one problem. Grace must take the form of freedom because many lack freedom or suffer from shame and oppression. The theme of liberation is basic to the New Testament, receives attention in Irenaeus, Athanasius, and Luther, and was revived in the last century in a variety of ways. A modern artistic expression comes from the new Coventry Cathedral where St. Michael binds the devil in chains.

The Purposes of God

5. The third group of interpretations uses yet a different point of view: for them Jesus reveals God's purpose for the creation. Yet within this standpoint there are striking variations. In the case of Athanasius, the great fourth-century defender of the Nicene Creed, the key is the incarnation of the Word of God in Jesus Christ. If the true God did not enter this world and dwell among us, offering to all the possibility of new life in Christ, then we remain lost in a world of sin and violence, dominated by the powers of this world. So for Athanasius, the incarnation of the Word is the key for salvation. It was also the issue at stake in the debate with Arius over the Nicene Creed: that the true, living God is present in this world bestowing life.

6. In Anselm, the attempt to find a rationale for the incarnation, leading to the death and resurrection of Jesus, can have no solution unless we affirm that it was necessary for God to *restore the creation*. Often misunderstood and maligned, Anselm invokes the medieval idea of honor, which refers to the multiple relations between the monarch and all those owing allegiance. Anselm uses the image to speak of the relations of God to all parts of the world, which reveal God's goodness. Sin, however, disrupts the harmony between humans and God. Like Athanasius, Anselm is motivated by the concern: What was God to do? God's honor must be restored but only God can accomplish this work of redemption. Thus we are drawn to the necessity of the incarnation. While Anselm repeatedly uses the word satisfaction, at no point does he move toward the idea of penal substitution where God demands a death in payment of sin. Rather, Jesus' death is an act of fidelity which restores on earth true humanity. Thus Jesus simultaneously conquers the devil and stands as the True Adam, inviting believers into his new humanity. We need to bear in mind that the word satisfaction can have positive and negative uses. If this is hard to comprehend, consider this question: Is God satisfied with the world as it is? If you think not, then you may be able to grasp Anselm's vision of God becoming human in order to restore the universe.

7. But Athanasius and Anselm do not exhaust the possibilities of starting with the purpose of God to interpret Jesus. In Schleiermacher,

the coming of Jesus is no accident, nor is it simply a response to sin. It is rather the *completion of the creation*. God intended from all time to become incarnate in Jesus and to bestow the Spirit on the church. There is but one eternal decree which wills the redemption brought by Jesus Christ and is mediated through the community of new life in his name. Here again we see a reliance on incarnation to interpret Jesus. What is also distinctive is that Schleiermacher offers the first great attempt to translate the ontological language of substance and persona of the early church into the historical, personal, and social language of the modern world. While he has been the source of much controversy, he also stands as the great exemplar of Christocentric theology in the nineteenth century.

Reconciliation

8. The aforementioned interpretations, however, do not exhaust the ways Jesus is interpreted. Three interpretations see the key in some form of reconciliation. In one, the true knowledge of God has been lost as we have given our trust and loyalty to idols of this world. This approach relies strongly on the Old Testament assumption that to know God is to love and serve God. There can be no true relation to God as long as we have turned from God, forgotten that our lives are dependent upon God and violated the commandments. Since a renewal of the covenant can only occur through the destruction of the idols and repentance, God must first appear as the sovereign who judges and stands against a sinful people. If one uses this imagery to interpret Jesus, then his life and death become an unveiling of our opposition to God and our betrayal of God's Kingdom. But the cross is not only a word of judgment against the world, it is also a word of grace leading to reconciliation. In this way Jesus is the light of the world: He exposes the idols. He is also the Way of God to us and the Way for us to God. Such an approach has both a prophetic and priestly quality. In the last century, renowned for its warfare and idolatry, H. Richard Niebuhr used this theme to describe the gospel as judgment and grace.

9. In Paul's First Letter to the Corinthians we find the image of *reconciliation* applied to divisions based on claims to spiritual power, wisdom and moral goodness. This is the only place in the New

Testament where ideological conflict is addressed directly as a comprehensive interpretation of Jesus. The theme is developed as follows: Jesus' death appears to be the victory of the world's claims to wisdom and power. But God vindicates Jesus in the resurrection, revealing that the weakness and foolishness of the cross are stronger than the world's power and wisdom. But why bring this up when writing to the divided Corinthians? Paul's point is that all claims to wisdom and power eventually lead to the crucifixion of the innocent. In dividing the church by claims to superiority, they are repeating the crucifixion of Jesus. Suddenly the image of the cross/crucifixion of Jesus becomes a universal symbol for the death of the innocent at the hands of those making claims. For Paul, therefore, the cross is both a judgment against the world and an act of grace. Only by giving up all worldly claims and claiming Jesus can we be reconciled in the face of our prejudices and divisions. The church is constituted not on the basis of our claims to religious correctness or moral goodness, but solely on the basis of God's will to reconcile us in spite of who and what we are. Reconciliation, therefore, can only be seen as a gift to a divided world.

10. Finally, Jesus may be interpreted with the image of *wondrous love*. This view is identified with Abelard, who develops it with great simplicity and force. If we are going to conclude that Jesus is a demonstration of the love of God, then let us simply say so. In spite of Gustaf Aulen's charge that nothing happens, Abelard does in fact affirm that love comes to earth in order to create a people who are bound together as brothers and sisters in the liberty of love. Thus the world shall be redeemed by the love of God mediated through the church. Wondrous love also becomes, in my view, the overarching theme for the theology of John Wesley. To be sure, Wesley uses many of the images named above and they all find their way into the hymns of Charles Wesley. But if one asks regarding God's motivation and our response to the hearing of the gospel, the answer for both questions is love. In the twentieth century we find an unexpected application of wondrous love in the work of Jurgen Moltmann. It is his contention that this century represents such horrendous destruction of innocent life that it is humankind that is outraged against God. It is God who is on trial. This prompts Moltmann to see in the

story of Jesus' crucifixion the presence of God. God's response to the suffering of humankind is to endure crucifixion as a demonstration of love.

Is it possible for there to be more than ten interpretations of Jesus' life, death, and resurrection? Absolutely! After publication of *Saving Power* the work of Rene Girard was brought to my attention. This perspective certainly deserves mention, especially since several writers have used his basic idea to develop their own views of Jesus.[4] Girard employs a theory of ritual sacrifice involving scapegoats, whereby a community rids itself of what is despised and threatening. To apply this to Jesus means that Jesus dies the death of the innocent scapegoat in order to bring an end to all violence used to protect society. This theory is definitely a distinct interpretation of Jesus and should not be confused with the views found in the Letter to the Hebrews or those relying on the general experience of sacrifice.

It is liberating to discover that these interpretations of Jesus complement one another rather than conflict. Since they describe different forms of grace addressed to different issues, one does not have to choose one over the others. And of course, the traditions have not done so in order to witness to the fullness of grace. In every tradition one finds many images used together, often woven into a larger tapestry. This variety of images grows out of multiple theological interests and practices in communities divided by space and time. These many interpretations of the cross reveal the way Christians understand their relation to Christ. The interpretations describe what Jesus has done for us, but they also describe how we understand ourselves in our sin and new life. They give substance to worship, the life of prayer, preaching, and education. They also affect the practice of the community: the relations between members and their interactions with the world. In Chapters 5 and 6 we will extend this discussion of how these theories form faith and life of communities.

All of this lifts up the necessity for clarity and conviction regarding the church's interpretation of Jesus as the basis for the church's proclamation—to its members and to the world. In this sense, every community faces a fundamentally Christological question: do we have anything to say

---

4. Cf. Bartlett, *Cross Purposes: The Violent Grammar of Christian Atonement*; Heim, *Saved From Sacrifice: A Theology of the Cross*.

about Jesus' life, death, and resurrection? More than any other, this issue exposes the crisis in mainline Protestants. For several decades preachers and teachers have lived with the fear that penal substitution is the only theory of atonement. This has paralyzed mainline churches in their efforts to proclaim Christ, lest they appear to support a message about a God being appeased by the suffering and blood of the innocent Jesus. If there is no alternative to this story of punishment and death, how does one speak of the cross? Lacking an answer, the cross is avoided and in its place we find moral admonitions, self-help advice, and a general message of love, which Americans interpret in terms of cultural ideas of love. By recovering the fullness of grace in many interpretations of the cross, the church is encouraged to return to its only treasure: the good news of Jesus Christ. Sorting out the various theories is in one sense a quest for *clarity*: just what do these images mean and how are they different from one another? Put in another way, can they function in the church as truly evangelical statements and do they express our most fundamental affirmations regarding God? Given the variety of images in the New Testament, it is clear that the earliest churches spent considerable time searching for clarity. Why else would they speak of Jesus in so many different ways? Clarity regarding what Jesus does allows us to regain *conviction* regarding Jesus Christ: that God has in fact done something for the salvation of the world in the story of Jesus. Put another way: Jesus really does make a difference. The church was born and received life in the conviction that Jesus is the agent of God who changes our lives. This conviction must be on our lips and find expression in our actions.

The Church's Identify and Life:
Reconsidering the Marks of the Church

Thus far we have explored the proposal that the church's self-understanding and life have been formed by the new life in Jesus Christ. This means: first, new life is a gift and promise from God; second, the church continues to exist as a community of new life only through the presence of Christ and the Spirit. Once one understands how origin and continuation are joined together, we reach a point where we may rightly understand the classic marks of the church. To speak of them outside of this context is misleading. It too easily suggests that these are attributes or characteristics of the church itself and not descriptions of God's gift and promise. What distinguishes the church can only be understood in a Christological context. In this context these traditional affirmations can give insight into the nature of the church.

What is meant by *marks* of the church? The many uses of the word *mark* are suggestive: A mark can be a boundary—a point which might be helpful in deciding what is and what is not the church. The word mark can refer to sign or symbol—again suggesting that the marks of the church represent its true being. Another suggestive meaning is a "brand, label, seal or tag put on an article to show owner, maker, etc.: as a trade-mark."[5] Here we have a rich mix of images drawn from commerce, the work of craftsmen and artisans, or any person wishing to claim ownership. If we play with these images one might ask: Are the marks of the church God's brand or label, identifying it as God's own people? Do the marks set the church apart as God's creation? Are the marks a seal placed upon the church by God—to remind the church and the world what the church is? Recall that the word seal is used extensively in the liturgy and discussions of the sacraments as signs and seals of God's grace. These explorations provide an imaginative introduction to the discussion, especially since they emphasize that the marks points to the gift and promise of God.

The Nicene Creed (381) declares that we believe "in one, holy, catholic and apostolic church."[6] Following Luther and Calvin, Claude Welch argued that in reciting the creed, one does not properly affirm belief *in* the church, since we are called to believe in God.[7] If we adopt this view, then this article of the creed allows us to affirm what we believe *about* the church. In what way, then, is it helpful to affirm that the church is one, holy, catholic and apostolic?

One

Among mainline Protestant churches, the burning issue for several decades is how shall we incorporate variety into churches that are so white and middle class. Thus we have gone through extensive changes and upheavals to celebrate the diversity of God's people according to gender,

5. *Webster's New Word Dictionary of the American Language*, 898.

6. Cf. Leith, *Creeds of the Churches*, 33.

7. Welch, *The Reality of the Church*, 42.

age, race, and ethnicity. Even more threatening has been the exposure of deep divisions along social, moral, and political lines, dealing with sexual orientation, war and peace, and the equality of women. Many denominations were confronted with their own forms of the culture war. All of these developments raised the more serious question: what is the basis of our unity? Diversity is a given in the human condition and in this world it plays out in cold and hot wars. To be sure, it is a good thing to break stereotypes regarding the Christian life and liberate those who are not allowed to stand as equals at the table of the Lord. But the more we become aware that we are different, the more the question is raised: on what basis do we stand at the table of the Lord as equals?

The question cannot be answered if we approach it from what Paul calls "a human point of view" (2 Cor 5:16). Such a perspective has been the reason some seek to elevate themselves and lower others. It condones the self-interest that prompts some to see others as things to be used. It reacts to what we do not understand with fear and prejudice. As a result, churches are separated and divided, displaying a miserable record trying to decide who belongs to the community. All of this gives cause for ridicule from outsiders and sorrow among some insiders.

Given this situation, it might be best to see the affirmation of oneness as a judgment against ourselves. The church can be one only as a gift of Christ to his people, a promise actualized in their gathering at Christ's table. But since they bring to the table all of their disagreements and longstanding divisions, in what sense are they united? Here I think Paul speaks to the issue in the clearest way. In his First Letter to the Corinthians, Paul describes a church divided by loyalty to different leaders, views of spirituality, moral practices, rivalries, and bad practices. (The list could well be used to describe the historic divisions among Christians.) Like an outraged parent, Paul could have simply reprimanded them and threatened them with a pending visit. But instead he speaks of the confrontation of the cross with the wisdom and power of the world. The Corinthians, no doubt, must have wondered what such a broad topic has to do with them. They did not have to wait long. Paul's point is simply this: Jesus was crucified by the good intentions of those wishing to protect truth and the moral order. But since they killed an innocent man, something is wrong. God uses the death of the innocent to expose the foolishness and weakness of the world's claims. Applied to the Corinthians, their claims to good theology, spiritual freedom, and special virtue are only producing division. In effect, they are like the powers which crucified Jesus in order to maintain their interests and sense of order. As with Corinth, so with us: the basis of our unity, is not in us or what we do or bring to the table, but in the new status God gives us in Christ. This is what it means to say salvation is a gift.

From this perspective the church is a new creation in a hostile and divided world. The sense of this new reality is illustrated in the passing of the peace of Christ: in the peace given to us by Christ members are united, but not on the basis of their claims but in spite of who or what they are. The oneness of the church is real—it is not imagined, not a future event, and definitely not something we will get to if we all try to work together—because it is in Christ. Thus we can say what everyone knows: apart from Christ and the life formed by him, Christians have very little in common. They differ by gender, race, language, sexual orientation, political, and social views. Sometimes they do not like one another very much. But the unity is still there—as a judgment against our hardness of heart and a promise of new life. It is one of the trademarks God has put on the people of the new covenant: that in the face of disagreement, anger and the most serious conflict, there is a way to be united in this world in the grace of God.

To confess the oneness of the church on these terms is to step back from the dominant American view of the church. The American Constitution launched the great experiment of religious freedom. This meant that individuals may choose to be religious and develop their religious interests in whatever way they wish. The definition of the church that has emerged is that of a voluntary association of like minded people. From a political and sociological perspective, this makes some sense, since that is largely how churches function. But from the standpoint of the church's origin, it makes no sense at all. The church is not a voluntary association brought into being by mutual interests, but a community of God's gift and promise. Furthermore, from a practical perspective it is now abundantly clear that the church is *not* like-minded. As was argued in the Introduction, the attempt to resolve the problem by gaining agreement on essentials does not work, since today everything may be considered an essential.

There has also been little success in trying to enforce or maintain unity by expelling those who disagree. No matter how many times churches divide and/or remove dissenters, new disagreements are soon present. This is especially the case over time, as younger generations gradually reveal a shift in world view or theological perspective. The fact is that the church of agreement is dead. To be sure, some refuse to admit this and still pursue the strategy that unity can be found by enforcing agreement. But in pursuing this strategy the church mirrors the world: status and worth are bestowed only on like-minded persons; those who disagree must be rejected or demonized.

In a time when congregations and denominations have destroyed themselves in search of unity based on agreement, one can only pray that we will claim the gift offered in the unity of Christ. In the oneness of Christ we find a new way of being at peace with one another, not based on who we are or what we bring, but on the claim of Christ laid upon us. To be united in Christ is to see one another as a brother or sister also claimed by Christ. I may express my opinions regarding them and even disagree with them, but I can not exclude them from the claim of Christ. We are united in this in spite of all of our preferences and our special claims. To affirm that the church is one is to affirm and receive our unity as a gift.

Holy

In what sense dare we speak of the church as holy? Our experience of all branches of Christianity reveals communities caught up in the warfare of this world, prone to compromise the cause of Christ, and weighed down by every imaginable sin. To be sure, not all Christians share this critical perspective. But before we deal with that, let us begin with the basic question: in what sense in the church holy?

Consider this story. When a pastor asked a group of college students "Are you saved?" no one responded. This was surprising because the students came from churches with strong religious commitments. They later explained their hesitation by saying that being saved implied some kind of moral perfection or special status, which they were reluctant to claim. They were also mindful of people who claimed to be saved but spoke and acted in ways quite contrary to Christ. In the discussion I proposed that they might think of the question relating to God's act in Christ rather than their personal achievements. If God has accepted and forgiven me by grace and claimed me for new life, then I am obligated to answer the question in the affirmative.

This suggests two things: First, if there is holiness in our lives, it is a gift of God in Christ. It is not our achievement or creation. Our real or imagined achievements are not the basis of our standing before God or the means to elevate ourselves over others. Holiness is something to be received in humility and with joy, but not with self-righteous pride. This obviously breaks with conventional wisdom that God loves us when we do good things and is angry with us when we do bad things. Christians are always tempted to mirror the dogma of the world that we get what we deserve. But Paul declares that God loves us while we were yet sinners. In other words, no one is pure and sinless; the only way to new life is through admitting that we do not have it and can only receive it as a gift. So Luther declares that whatever righteousness we have is alien to us; it is the righteousness of Christ.[8]

Second, the holiness of the church and its members consists of the gifts of Christ and the Spirit: faith, hope, love, peace, kindness, forgiveness, joy, freedom, gratitude, suffering, and rejoicing with one another, and speaking the truth regarding justice and peace. These qualities of life are signs of healing and wholeness in a violent and fractured world. They are the things which make up the being of the church and the Christian life. They flow from Christ and the Spirit through the members, as individuals and the community grow toward the maturity of Christ.

When we confess the church is holy, we are pointing to the action of God in our lives. We affirm that in endless ways, our lives are sustained by gifts of the Spirit through the nurture and witness of those around us. But now the hard part. This can and must be affirmed without insisting that the church has reached perfection and is without sin. Such a self-critical perspective assumes that the struggle with sin is not finished and that even those baptized in Christ are still subject to the temptations of sin and the idols of this world. This is what Paul means when he declares that we are simultaneously redeemed and yet sinful. It also assumes that sin is not a matter of ignorance or mistakes, but of self-love and rebellion against God, that is, a state of mind and heart that is never totally overcome in this life. This is indeed a most serious view of sin. But we need to bear in

8. Cf. Luther, "Two Kinds of Righteousness," 86–97.

mind that it was never used to deny the advent of holiness in our lives or the possibility of change. Rather, it is needed to remind us that even the new life involves the struggle between sin and forgiveness. From this perspective, then, one can speak of both the presence of holiness and the failings of the church.

But not all Christians share this realism regarding the church and the Christian life. Roman Catholics are more apt to see the church as an extension of the incarnation of Christ, thereby elevating the church to a higher level of being. Thus it can make bold claims about the infallibility of papal pronouncements and resist charges that the church itself is caught up in sin. From a different perspective, Anabaptists and Pentecostals also tend to be more optimistic about the church. Relying upon the transformative power of believers' baptism and the bestowal of the Spirit, these groups tend, in different degrees, to see Christians crossing over into a new life. By contrast, Lutherans and Calvinists tend to affirm the realism described above, which means they are not likely to claim perfection for the church. But even here, when these groups become more and more dogmatic and authoritarian, they lose their willingness to speak of the pervasiveness of sin and the corruptibility of all things. If convinced of their righteousness, they may assume the church, the state, or the corporation is exempt from judgment.

The differences among Christians regarding the presence of sin in the church will emerge again in our discussion of strategies for change. In many respects it is one of the most serious dividing points among Christian traditions.

Catholic

The concept *catholic* contains a cluster of ideas, but how they are defined and where the emphasis is placed is somewhat illusive. More than any other mark of the church, catholic appears to contain the claim of legitimacy. This is clear when The Roman Catholic *Catechism* defines catholic to mean: first, that Christ is fully present in every church; second, the church has been sent into the whole world and thus includes or is open to all humanity; third, connection to the apostolic succession extending to the Bishop of Rome. A fourth idea, implied in all three but deserving attention, is the visible church, representing the Incarnate Christ to the world.[9]

With the exception of the Roman claim to apostolic succession, Protestants affirm these ideas, giving emphasis on openness to all people. Consider the work of the World Council of Churches in 1968: to be catholic is to participate in the fullness of life in Christ.[10] The catholic church has integrity (i.e., unity and completeness), as a gift of the Spirit. Catholicity finds expression in worship which is open to ". . . all sorts and conditions of men and women . . . ," as well as the continuity of faith, liturgy, service, and witness through the ages and around the world.[11] Further light is shed on the meaning of catholic by what is denied. The opposite of catholic is egoism and particularism.[12] Catholicity is denied by anything which divides, excludes, or separates humanity.

The emphasis on openness and diversity in the World Council document has been embraced in many ways by Protestants. Consider the practice of substituting the word *universal* for *catholic*, emphasizing the need for openness to all people throughout the world—as a reality and a goal. As such, the redefined use of catholic becomes a defense of diversity. That is, the catholic church consists of many branches or denominations, which are parts of a larger whole. It is precisely because they differ that each has a unique value. This leads to the further conclusion that the true church could only be envisioned as the unity of all of the parts, where each part brings its special gifts to the gathering.

To define catholic as the sum of diverse parts, however, can lead to unintended consequences. If each specific denomination is only a part of the larger whole, does this mean it is incomplete? Some would quite willingly agree, since they wish to praise diversity, using Paul's image of the Body of Christ. But for an Eastern Orthodox like John Meyendorf, this is an intolerable view of catholicity, since it implies that the parts are not truly catholic.[13] According to Meyendorf, catholicity affirms the presence of Christ in the church and Christ can only be fully present. To believe in

9. *Catechism of the Catholic Church: With Modifications from the Editio Typica,* 239–47.

10. Leith, "The Holy Spirit and the Catholicity of the Church," 590.

11. Ibid., 590–91.

12. Ibid., 590.

13. Meyendorff, *Catholicity and the Church,* 55.

the catholic Church, therefore, is to affirm that wherever the church is, it is truly the church because Christ is truly present.

In general, I find this critique of the Protestant application of catholicity to be compelling. We ought to find another way to defend diversity without implying that each church is incomplete. But greater clarity is needed for what the Roman Catholic *Catechism* and the Eastern Orthodox mean by the real presence of Christ. When one explores this issue, one discovers that a great deal is packed into this phrase. The World Council document may be instructive in this regard, when it declares that catholicity expresses "the fullness, integrity, and the totality of life in Christ."[14] This opens up the discussion in dramatic ways. It is not simply Christ's presence per se which is being affirmed, but the entire story of salvation. In Paul we already see the mutual participation of all of humanity in Christ's death and resurrection, as well as his participation in our life. As the True Adam, he restores humanity to its intended goal. When the early church combines this idea with John's affirmation of the Word made flesh, it moves toward the creedal affirmation that Jesus Christ is the Word incarnate, the union of God and humanity. The new life, therefore, is human existence as God intended, lived in Christ and the Spirit. It is not the denial of our humanity, but its true and complete expression. When we return to the debate over catholic, this gives new meaning to the emphasis on Christ's presence in the church. The Christ who is present already contains all of humanity—not all particular people, but the true form of all people. As the incarnate Word, he also represents God's embrace of the creation. The world transformed and redeemed is now present, or visible, for all to see. It is against this background that one must rightly claim that catholic means: 1) that Christ is truly present in every church, 2) that because true humanity is already in Christ, therefore the church is open to all people; 3) the affirmation of the church as a visible community with structures made of wood and stone, forms of organization and regular practices.

This interpretation of catholic makes clear that what is at stake here is not an abstract affirmation of Christ's presence, or even a contentious claim of legitimacy by one church against others. It is instead a bold confession of our salvation by God in Christ. Particular churches in time and place are not what they seem to be from a worldly perspective: ordinary

14. Leith, *The Holy Spirit,* 590.

people, buildings created by human hands, or an amalgam of activities and programs. They are the people and things of this world which God has chosen to invest with saving power. It is this claim, deeply rooted in the theology of the incarnation of the Word, which goes to the heart of catholicity. The incarnation was not a flash of lightening but the continuing presence of God in this world. That presence continues through the risen Christ, who is Lord of the Church, and the Holy Spirit, which gives life to the church. All this can be said without claiming that the church is an extension of the incarnation.[15] Christ is present in the church as a gift and through the Spirit sustains its faith and life.

Distracted by inter-church wars over which is the true church, Protestants are usually not predisposed to affirm such a strong view of catholicity. It would be helpful if they could appropriate the commitment for this perspective found in John Williamson Nevin and Philip Schaff, the two great representatives of the Mercersburg Theology.[16] For them catholic represented the church as the embodied Word in time and place. Like the incarnation, the word catholic signaled two things: that Christ was truly present in the church and that humanity is drawn into unity with God. Nevin was particularly concerned to reject the view that the church is a collection of individual parts, since this denied our solidarity in both sin and salvation. Because Christ is the union of humanity as a whole, the church is a community united in Christ and open to all people. It stood for the necessity of the church to be a human institution, proclaiming the Word and celebrating the sacraments.[17] This attempt to speak of catholic as a positive element in the church's life brought Nevin and Schaff under heavy criticism as being pro-Roman and not true Protestants. Nevertheless their point is valid and a necessary corrective to the modern liberal view that Christianity is a set of ideas or the sectarian tendency to divide into separate churches. To affirm the catholic church is to believe that it is possible and necessary for Christ to be embodied in communities of faith and life. It is to say, using the terms developed here,

15. Welch, 117–22. Welch is persuasive in arguing for a likeness and congruity between the union of the divine and human in Christ with the relation of Christ and the church, but that they are not the same.

16. For those unfamiliar with Nevin and Schaff, consider: "The Anxious Bench" 9–126, and *The Mystical Presence*, and Schaff, *The Principle of Protestantism*.

17. Cf. the discussion of Nevin's view of catholicity in Littlejohn, *The Mercersburg Theology and the Quest for Reformed Catholicity*, 147–69.

that the gift and promise are actually in this world and present for all to receive. This can be affirmed without adopting the authoritarian claims of the Roman tradition or its claim to infallibility. It is not about claiming special privilege for one tradition, but claiming that in all times and places there is, or can be, the true church because Christ is truly present. Did Christ not promise this when ever two or three gather in his name?

Apostolic

All Christians claim to be apostolic. The problem is that they mean quite different things by such a claim. I have identified at least eight different views of apostolic which distinguish communities from one another.[18] But these definitions of apostolic can function in more than one way: Since they appeal to different aspects of faith and practice, they can be mutually exclusive alternatives. But for the same reason they can complement one another. We see this already occurring in some communities which appeal to more than one of the views. In some respects these eight perspectives come close to being what Chapter 2 will call norms, since they function as standards or guides for determining faith and practice. Consider these eight views of apostolic:

1. Participation in the sacramental life of the Historic Community. This view joins together three things: regular and faithful participation; the centrality of the sacraments; the claim of unbroken succession with the apostles. As is evident among Roman Catholics, Eastern Orthodox, and Episcopalians, this perspective involves high church liturgy, a strong emphasis on episcopal authority and reliance on church traditions.

2. Proclaiming the True Faith. Here the emphasis falls upon the protest against current practices and traditions of the institutional church and the necessity of renewal by the Word of God in Jesus Christ. Participation in the sacraments and acceptance of institutional au-

---

18. This typology of images of apostolic was first developed in *Christ the Reconciler: A Theology for Opposites, Differences, and Enemies*, 31–60. At the time it was presented as an alternative to the typology presented by Dulles, *Models of the Church*. I considered Dulles' effort to be flawed for two reasons: after presenting five models, several are criticized so severely that they are questionable; the models are drawn from theologians rather than actual church communities.

thority are subordinated to the authority of the gospel as found in Scripture. Proclamation is usually tied to a response of faith as trust of the heart.

3. Rebirth in the Spirit. In practice, if not in theory, the first two definitions can become preoccupied with institutional authority and/ or doctrinal disputes. Thus in nearly every age a protest has been offered in the name of the Holy Spirit. It is the Spirit which gives rebirth, opens our eyes to the true meaning of Scripture, and creates the fellowship of believers.

4. Acts of Love and Justice, or Right Action. The first three views tend to be concerned about the origin of the Christian life and our union with Christ. But what if the true mark of the church is found in acts of love and justice, as commanded in the Sermon on the Mount and Matthew 25? Using these passages and others regarding signs of love as the true test of fidelity to Christ, this perspective thinks of the apostolic church as the active agent of love and justice.

5. Confessing our Unity in Christ. Some Christians readily value what has been said thus far, but see the genuine mark of the apostolic church to be mission in the world for the sake of proclaiming the gospel. Here the incarnation marks the beginning of a new age, whereby God is uniting all things in Christ.

6. The Covenant Community or Gathered Church. One can value everything that has been said above and still not find the apostolic church, unless one participates in a disciplined community of faith, worship, fellowship, and service. This community stands against the state church, since it is called out of the world and, by its faith and practice, stands against the world.

7. Pilgrims and Seekers. This image calls believers to leave the security of formal and established systems of religion and journey as pilgrims and seekers. There is here a strong protest against claims to certainty in faith and practice, coupled with a strong preference for freedom, variety and the spiritual quest. If it is difficult to name whole denominations as representative of this view, it is quite easy to identify members of any congregation who prefer this model of apostolic—

and thereby provoke endless discussions over things most thought were settled.

8. Solidarity of Jesus with Those who Suffer. The image of liberation goes back to the New Testament and reappears in liberation theology. Broadly speaking, from this perspective the apostolic church is the church which identifies with Jesus who is already in the world in solidarity with those who suffer. Such a view leads to a different way of thinking about authority and the form of the church, though in its Roman Catholic version, it is tied to the affirmations of Trinity and Incarnation.

When one surveys these ways Christians claim to be apostolic, many things become clear. First, it is now apparent why churches claim to be catholic and apostolic, but only some base this upon unbroken succession of bishops back to the apostles. In fact, for all of the views except the first, such a claim is theologically irrelevant, though matters of continuity in faith and practice are quite relevant.

Second, the typology helps us understand how Christians can so strongly disagree. This is because they are appealing to different values. As already noted, the different views can complement one another if one is willing to see the church in more complex terms. One does not have to deny the importance of sacramental participation just because one stands with Luther in affirming the importance of proclaiming the Word. Thus the way is open for thinking about the apostolic church which would gather all of these together in a meaningful way to enrich the faith and life of the church.

Third, to do this, however, it will be necessary to cease using the different views of apostolic as tools for combat and warfare. For example, if you take your favorite view of apostolic, extol its positive formulation, and contrast it with the negative forms of the other seven, you win the argument. Since all eight have positive and negative forms, it does not take much imagination to do this. In fact, many of us grew up in traditions where the distortions and excesses of other traditions were living proof that our choice was correct. Not only did we vow allegiance to our form of apostolic, but we also vowed never to be like the others. For example, as a Protestant loyal to Luther and Calvin, it was easy to defend such loyalty by pointing to the problems of Roman Catholic authoritarianism or the excesses of claims to the Spirit. So it is that we still carry the baggage from those inter-church wars, so intent on maintaining the purity of our apostolic vision, even though it cut one off from other genuine forms of apostolicity. But the fact is that those wars must cease, partly because they involved ignoring the distortions of one's own tradition, and partly because they perpetuated the divisions of the people of Christ. The great gift of the Spirit in our time is to see the opportunity to claim the faith and practice of multiple views of apostolic.

General Conclusions

We began the chapter with a view of the formation of the church by God's action in Jesus Christ. In spite of their misunderstandings, doubts and denials, the first believers are formed into a community. By grace they receive healing, new life and peace with God and one another. It was necessary to begin in this way because what develops flows from this originating experience of Jesus' life, death and resurrection. The images of Jesus seek to interpret these events. What comes to be called the marks of the church really are about what God has done in Jesus Christ in the community. Only after we have some sense of the primacy of grace and the intervention of holiness can we understand the marks of the church. Once all these things are before us, it should not surprise us that the marks of the church can also be interpreted in diverse ways. This is especially the case with the claim to apostolicity.

Each mark from the Nicene Creed affirms that the church exists only by God's gift and promise.

- The church is united and reconciled by Christ. It is a re-presentation of the oneness of God and humanity.

- The church embodies by grace the new life of Christ: the healing of forgiveness and the peace of Christ. In its life and witness it demonstrates the presence of holiness in this world.

- The church is a community drawn from many times and places because Christ is present wherever believers gather. It is catholic in its embrace of life with Christ in this world.

- The church is apostolic by demonstrating patterns of grace to its members and the world.

Finally, we began by describing how a community came into being through the formative power of God's act in Jesus Christ. We then began to uncover how Christians experience God's saving power in diverse ways. A similar conclusion arose out of the analysis of the marks of the church: all of the marks, but especially apostolicity, inspire different forms of life and practice. Thus we can now begin to understand how the church is formed by Jesus Christ, as well as how it includes multiple formations resulting in a richness of traditions. This analysis will become crucial in later chapters where a specific proposal is made to explain the great diversity of churches.

Case Study: When Unity and Holiness Collide.

In the fall of 1962 a Vatican spokesman declared in a public lecture at Harvard University that Protestants were *separated brethren*. I heard these words as a dramatic change in the way Roman Catholics thought of Protestants. If it seems quite mild in today's climate, think of the words as an alternative to *heretics*. We have indeed come a long way with regard to theological disputes, as denominations become more willing to accept the variety of doctrinal views and affirm some form of unity. The reasons for this are many: families have been forced to live with variety due to intermarriage and individuals find themselves working with people of other traditions; churches have been greatly affected by the ecumenical theology and biblical studies of the twentieth century. This is not to say that every tradition still does not have a set of convictions which it considers to be non-negotiable. Likewise, there are still some traditions which require complete agreement on the entire list of doctrines held to be sacred. Nevertheless, considerable progress has been made regarding accepting major differences within traditions and between traditions when it comes to doctrinal matters.

The situation is quite different when it comes to moral issues. While all Christians may affirm, in some way, that baptized Christians still sin and fall short of the true holiness of the Spirit, they differ greatly as to the progress one should make toward sanctification. Stated in the negative, they disagree on what actions are unacceptable for membership. As a result, there is no agreement about the magnitude of particular sins. Nor is there a consistent pattern of rules regarding social policies. For example, consider the changes and variations in practice regarding slavery, attitudes toward women, monarchy, military service, divorce, and usury. The matter is further complicated by the fact that Christianity assumes failure to achieve holiness: it insists that we acknowledge that we sin and builds into its worship a rite of confession and forgiveness.

One development in the early church is instructive: Writing toward the end of the second century, Tertullian assumes that entrance to the church by repentance and baptism places on the believer the requirement not to sin. But as we examine his discussion, it would appear that in this context sin refers to major failings (probably, murder, adultery, and idolatry), though only a few are actually mentioned: eating meat offered to idols, perverse teaching, and adultery. According to Tertullian, these can be forgiven in a second act of repentance and forgiveness, but that is the limit.[19] He implies that this limit was so feared that some put off revealing their sins, since they would then be living in jeopardy of exclusion lest it happen again. The very process of this second forgiveness was no less threatening: it required public confession and humiliation by means of sack cloth and ashes in front of the congregation.[20] While it is risky to assume that any one practice was universal among churches spread out around the Mediterranean, we may venture several conclusions from this text: First, there appears to be a distinction, though undefined, between minor and major sins. While this sounds reasonable, it is difficult to maintain, given Jesus' insistence that sins of the heart are serious violations. Furthermore, it is going to be very difficult to reach unanimity regarding what are the major sins. (Tertullian includes trusting in excessive riches among major sins, but how would that be defined and enforced?) Second, it will be difficult to restrict forgiveness to two times. To be sure, Matthew 18 endorses exclusion of an unrepentant sinner, but elsewhere Jesus commands that we forgive seventy times seven, i.e., continuously.

This brief excursion into the early church highlights the difficulties of trying to name unforgivable sins and/or required social policies. Yet in the past two centuries, American Christians have split repeatedly over these matters on issues of slavery and race, women's rights, alcohol, divorce, war, abortion, and sexual orientation. In effect, the bonds of unity have not been strong enough to withstand conflicting views of holiness. And,

19. Tertullian, *Treatises on Penance*, 27–29.
20. Ibid., 31–37.

we must note, it is not just the conservatives who insist on compliance with a standard of holiness; liberals are just as likely to require agreement on moral issues as a requirement for unity. In the face of this collision between unity and holiness, several comments are appropriate.

The first is that all sides are very selective in making out the list of requirements. Selective in the sense that it could be much longer, since there are at least a hundred moral and social issues on which Christians disagree. It is also selective in the sense that at the present time, Christians are willing to insist on correct behavior regarding one or two, but show little interest in others. For example, both sides in the debates over abortion and homosexuality do not, in general, show the same zeal regarding peace making or divorce. So we need to ask why any one of these issues becomes the decisive issue for our time. In fact, why do believers and their churches feel so strongly about one or two of these issues that they will gladly make it a matter of separating from other Christians?

Some will answer by declaring that abortion and homosexuality are the great moral issues of our day. But so are women's rights, war, ecology, health, and the safety of children. This response only drives us back to ask: why are these issues more important than others? This prompts others to reply that abortion and homosexuality are decisive issues because of mandates in Scripture. While there are indeed several verses of Scripture which speak against homosexual acts, it is not clear how these passages are to be used. Simply put, they fall into the broad area of moral admonitions relating to individual and social practices. The Bible, however, contains such a wide range of rules and admonitions that no church accepts all of them. Some of the things relate to practices which are no longer accepted, such as polygamy or the death penalty for minor infractions. Some relate to dietary and social practices. Others relate to political and economic practices which we have set aside. The Bible also presents us with an ancient view of the world's origin and a cosmology where a flat earth is the center of the universe. Yet few today wish to insist upon these views of the world. What these things mean is that it is not always self-evident what conclusion is to be drawn because something is sanctioned or prohibited in the Bible. Consider the matter this way: should the verses condemning homosexuality be classified with the list of things we no longer consider, for various reasons, to be binding, or, shall these verses be put on the same status with Jesus' teachings in the Sermon on the Mount?

This is not a trivial question, nor one raised with malicious intent. In America we do not feel obligated to be ruled by a monarchy, even though portions of the Bible sanction such a form of government. Most Christians accept, to some degree, divorce, even though it is condemned by Jesus. These two examples make it plain that most of the people claiming to accept the Bible as binding do not in fact do so. What complicates the debate over homosexuality is that both sides appeal to Scripture as if all one needed is a verse from Scripture to settle a matter. But this seldom works, as is evident by the debates over war, women's rights, or slavery. What is needed in debates like the one over homosexuality is for both sides to indicate why certain verses of Scripture should or should not be binding for the church today. For example, conservatives need to explain whether all of the strange and excessive rules of the Bible should be enforced if we are to accept the prohibitions against homosexuality. Conversely, liberals need to explain how, if they reject specific verses, anything in the Bible is relevant.

If both sides in the debate over homosexuality would explain how they are using Scripture—specific verses and the entire book—we would probably come closer to an answer to the question raised: why make this question decisive? When each side revealed the norms and basic commitments used to evaluate this particular issue, it would become apparent that more is involved than several verses of Scripture. We would begin to see that there is a general perspective regarding the Bible and its role in the life of the community, traditions of faith and moral practice, as well as broad cultural traditions. These matters would probably give us more fruitful discussions than ones where the two sides trade verses of Scripture. This is said in recognition of the fact that on the issues of abortion and homosexuality, agreement has not been reached by appeals to specific verses of Scripture. The debate has also been politicized in very negative ways, often leading to violence. It is clear that in many situations, the demand for holiness has shattered any concern for unity.

It may well be that agreement will not be reached by debate, given the highly charged climate. Perhaps the only way any level of respect and understanding can be reached is through face-to-face conversation. It is at this point that the churches need to insist on strategies for conflict resolution that draw on the church's resources rather than the cultural strategies of power politics, separation, demonization, and violence. Churches should be insisting that we speak face to face, engage in prayer, study, and sharing the peace of Christ—even in the face of radical disagreement—over extended periods of time. In effect, the mandate for unity must be reaffirmed against the zeal for holiness.

But can we be united if we are not of the same mind on moral practices? There are some things that can not be reconciled with the unity and holiness of the church. For example, the exclusion of persons by virtue of their birth violates the affirmation that God created all people and that all are welcome at the table of the Lord. Recall that baptism has never been withheld from persons because of gender, race, age, ethnicity, class, or physical or mental disabilities. So I cannot imagine any church condoning slavery, violence, or genocide. But this still leaves us with the contentious issues like abortion and homosexuality. What shall we do? My immediate response is that we already belong to communities of faith where there is widespread disagreement on issues just as important: for example, war, the use of money, the environment, health, equality, or community. Why can we not live together and be together at the Lord's table in the face of disagreement on these two burning issues? Here we have an example of what was meant when it was argued earlier that we are united by Christ in the face of disagreement over things we take to be essential—not just in the face of little differences. The alternative is to divide the church one more time. But how many times are we to do that? Once divided, what will each side do with its children who disagree? Division and denunciation are the strategies of the world as it seeks to gain power over others. The church is called to be in the world in a different way: united in Christ even in the face of alternative claims to holiness.

two

Norms

The Second Essential Component:

The Church is a community which affirms norms for its faith and life.

The Role of Norms in Communities of Faith

WHEN YOU LISTEN CAREFULLY to what Christians say, it soon becomes evident that there is something guiding the discussion. Sometimes they refer back to it as if it were a starting point, which indeed it is. But herein lies a riddle: what appears to be the starting point is also derived from centers of authority already at work in the community. It can have no authority unless it gives expression to what the community takes to be essential. But once extracted from authorities such as the Bible, creed, or tradition, the idea serves as a guide for understanding the very authorities that gave it birth. Thus, while dependent on primary confessions and documents, the idea captures the essence of faith and life for the community. In this way it becomes the starting point as well as the guide, used to sort out what is most important from a multitude of ideas. It functions as the standard or rule, providing a framework for faith and action. It is, in effect, an organizing principle which allows one to set some things aside and add others. This then is what I mean by a *norm* for a community. It defines the faith and, of course, defines the community.

If we want an example, none stands out better than Martin Luther's use of the affirmation of justification by grace in Paul's letters. Time and again he returns to this as his starting principle and ultimate standard. While it appears to be based on a prior standard (namely, the authority of Scripture), in fact it is the other way around. Scripture has authority because it contains this affirmation and Luther will use it to sort out what is important in Scripture. He will also reorganize the life and practice of the church: two sacraments instead of seven, a new understanding of the Lord's Supper as a gift of grace, the revision of the homily into a sermon to proclaim grace, access to the Scripture with a Bible in the language of the people, a new hymnody, and a new catechism for teaching. Once Luther found the proclamation of grace to be the ultimate standard, then everything else could be sorted out and new patterns for the church could be created.

As one can imagine, there is more than one way Christians have formulated norms for faith and practice. The differences between Christians are not accidental, but rooted in the constellation of ideas, commands, and practices which generate norms. This, of course, makes it difficult to negotiate arguments between norms because each starts from a different place. Some Christians find it compelling to start with the traditions rooted in the church of the first five centuries and extending to the present through the guidance of church leaders. This is basically an episcopal norm, since it relies upon the bishops and is usually ultimately lodged in one, such as the Bishop of Rome or one of the Patriarchs of Eastern Orthodoxy. Other Christians gravitate toward finding the norm to be the Bible itself, as the Word of God set over against all other authorities of the church. Yet many who speak broadly about the Bible as the starting point actually rely upon a more specific norm within the Bible. The example of Luther illustrates the point. The Anabaptists also illustrate how specific portions of the Bible give meaning to the whole (in this case, Matt 5–7 and 18). In the past two hundred years others have taken those portions of the New Testament which refer to the final things to be the key. For them, calculations regarding the end time and descriptions of the last days govern thought and practice. Church tradition and Bible, however, do not exhaust the possibilities. A wide range of Christians would find their starting point in one or more aspects of the Christian life, be it new birth in the Spirit, acts of love, or the transition from sin to holiness. In the past fifty years the traditional image of liberation has been revived by many around the world as a way to express their affirmation of liberation from social, political, and economic domination. Finally, we might even refer to the way in which unions of church and state form a starting point for thinking about the church. For centuries this was the norm, though it took radically different forms in Eastern Orthodoxy, where the state held power over the church, in contrast to West, where the church often was either equal to the state or retained ultimate authority. In America, we appear to be free from a union of church and state, though some Christians speak boldly the language of a nation governed by the faith and practice of a conservative set of Christian rules. Among these groups the coalition of religion and the state, preserving the status quo against all change, appears to take precedence over any appeal to the Bible or doctrine.

Before proceeding, a word is needed regarding the relation of *norms* and the topic of the next chapter, i.e., *centers of authority*. The category *norm* is used here as a value or standard which both guides the community in its interpretation of what is authoritative and provides a self-definition of the community itself. Norms are drawn from centers of authority, but function as a guide for understanding general authorities, such as Bible, creed, or tradition. The governing norm becomes decisive for faith and practice in those cases where centers of authority stand in conflict. For these reasons, the discussion of norms is placed before that of centers of authority.

Given this perspective on the significance of a norm for a community of faith, as well as a brief survey of the range of options, we will now turn to a specific proposal for a normative principle. While it is rooted in the Reformation tradition, it also seeks to embrace the ecumenical perspective which has been so influential in the twentieth century. The presentation of this norm will also clarify how it is differentiated from the other options. It should be emphasized that in presenting this proposal, I am moving into the third form of analysis, namely, making a case for a preferred option. The proposal intends two things: On the one hand, the central categories are deliberately defined in such broad terms that it can be quite inclusive of ecumenical Protestants and Roman Catholics. On the other hand, for those who find that the central categories do not include them, then it should be understood as one option in the ongoing attempt to establish norms for the church. Making the case for this option does not imply that it is the *only* norm for Christian faith.

Reforming the Norm for Our Time

Let us begin with a classic definition of Protestants from 1845 by the church historian Phillip Schaff. In *The Principle of Protestantism*, Schaff sought to capture the essence of the reforms of Luther and Calvin. His presentation was divided into two parts, using the distinction of material and formal principles.[1] The former is the doctrine of justification by grace, the latter is the priority of the Bible. The one gives the specific substance of Protestant faith, whereas the other locates the general authority for such faith. If the Bible as a norm stands over against tradition, church leaders or reason, it still requires some key to unlock its central message. This is what the material principle does.

Schaff's presentation is a tour de force: it captures the genius of the Reformers by using the two great symbols *sola gratia* and *sola Scriptura*. This allows Schaff to do two things: affirm in positive terms the twofold principle guiding Protestants; use it as a critical tool against the traditional adversary (Roman Catholics) and the nineteenth-century challenges from rationalism and sectarianism in America. Time and again Protestants have looked to these principles for inspiration. They are embedded in our confessional documents, our worship and preaching, and many of us carry them in our hearts.

What is striking about Schaff's work is that he tells us quite clearly that it is dated. By mid-nineteenth century in America, Roman Catholics were no longer the greatest challenge to Protestants and the church once again needed to be reformed.[2] But we now live in the twenty-first century—not the sixteenth nor the nineteenth century. So faith must be re-defined for our time. As much I resonate with Schaff"s affirmation and analysis, it is difficult to simply repeat his definition if we are to follow his advice to speak for ourselves.

First, we need to recognize certain difficulties with the phrase *sola Scriptura*. This is a challenge because many in America see the Bible as a symbol of authority beyond the clamor of a world gone crazy and divided

---

1. Schaff, The Principle of Protestantism, 80–124.
2. Ibid., 80.

by partisan rivalries. TV evangelists for good reason hold the Bible in their hands, claim to believe it and quote it repeatedly. It is therefore tempting to outbid our opponents in a show of unqualified belief in the Bible. But in our time the Bible is the most abused of books. Most of us recoil in horror when someone says the Bible is like a *Sears Manual*, providing operating instructions for life, or when someone tries to score points by asking: "Do you believe every word of the Bible?" We still affirm *sola Scriptura* in the sense that it is the primary authority for faith and life. But we are also keenly aware that the Bible does not speak with one voice, that it is historically bound to ancient times and places, and that it requires interpretation. Even Luther did not consider every verse of equal significance, but admitted that he worked with a canon within the canon to interpret the Bible, aided by creeds and favorite theologians like Augustine. But this approach does not lend itself to sound bites. Nor do we agree on how to reformulate the war cry *sola Scriptura* in light of several centuries of historical-critical study. To continue to define the Protestant tradition by the symbol *sola Scriptura* only perpetuates the notion that Scripture by itself, in all of its parts, is the self-evident standard for faith. Schaff did not intend this, nor did Luther or Calvin. We are going to have to be more specific as to how Scripture is authoritative.

Second, this is precisely what has happened in modern theology. When modern theology faced all of the critical problems associated with Scripture, it chose to affirm the confession of saving power within Scripture rather than defend all of the words and verses of Scripture. That is to say, it shifted the focus from proving the faith on the basis of the inerrancy of Scripture to confessing faith in Jesus Christ, the agent of God in redeeming the world. Schleiermacher and Barth may represent rival ways of being Christocentric, but the fact is that they agree on defining Christian faith in relation to Jesus Christ. The Bible has authority because it witnesses to Jesus Christ. This shift is not a rejection of the Bible but a more precise affirmation regarding the basis of our faith. Furthermore, the more Luther and Calvin were read, the more it became apparent that they placed the emphasis on confessing Christ. They affirmed that the Bible can only be interpreted by the power of the Spirit in us. What is needed then, is a new way to affirm the primacy of Scripture without allowing it to be a substitute for the saving power of God in Jesus Christ.

Third, while it is commendable to affirm the primacy of justification by grace, Schaff's formulation creates a gulf between justification and sanctification. Only justification is mentioned in the material principle. This catches the eye because Lutherans and Reformed have struggled for centuries with the relation between the two principles. In fact, one might even say they are virtually paralyzed regarding sanctification. One reason for this is that we fear the legalism that tries to order our lives in the ways of holiness. The various attempts to instill the holy life by rules have not worked but instead have created division and sorrow. The reaction against legalism, however, is just as problematic. A liberal culture readily affirms unconditional love, finding great comfort in hearing that love accepts us as we are. To be sure, it is quite counter-cultural to affirm a love that is not based on achievement or seeks a return on investment. There is indeed something extravagant and risky about God's acceptance of the prodigal son, in spite of the outrage of the self-righteous brother. But as this plays out in American religion, it too easily becomes what Bonhoeffer called cheap grace: God loves you and you don't have to respond in any way. It is all gift with no response to the promise of new life. The matter is not easily resolved, as we shall see in later discussions. But here it needs to be said that the wording of the fundamental norm ought to build a bridge from justification to sanctification, rather than treat them as separate topics.

Fourth, justification by grace in our time has become synonymous with the forgiveness of sins. This of course is one of the major forms of grace as affirmed in the gospels and the interpretations of Jesus. But it is not the only form of grace, as I have argued in *Saving Power*. We diminish the gospel if we confine it to one form of saving power, such as forgiveness of sins, in contrast to liberation or reconciliation. Likewise, we restrict the Eucharist by having the liturgy be primarily concerned with forgiveness of sins, as is presently the case. A more evangelical proclamation would present us with a wider range of liturgies for the Eucharist, reflecting the seasons of the church year as well as many ways grace renews life in this world. The problem with focusing entirely on forgiveness of sins is that this theme has developed into a highly individualistic form of religion. It is what I call the great American heresy: you can believe in God but you don't have to belong to a church. American religion is so infected with this individualism that it is not clear how we can escape from its influence.

This ought to warn us that when we formulate the norm for our time, we must affirm a communal form of faith and life.

These concerns are the grounds for proposing that we need to re-define the norm in a new way for our time. Schaff himself urged us to name the dangers we face in American society as we seek to be faithful to Christ. Let us begin by naming the powers of this world that challenge the Christian faith: A secular society tempts us to see the world as if that is all there is. It is as if the world were *flat*, that is, lacking any depth, transcendence or mystery. In such a world the preoccupation with sur-vival and work—whether by necessity or choice—becomes paramount, followed closely by the drives for pleasure and success. Our culture also knows no bounds in the exclusion of persons based on race, class, ethnic origin, gender, sexual orientation, and now immigration status. We are programmed to think of human relations in terms of power and violence. These mark our social and political history, but all too often characterize family life. American culture assumes that these forces can be reconciled to Christian faith and that we must accommodate ourselves to them. On a regular basis the news media bring us stories about how anyone who questions these forces is a godless anti-Christian. If this is the culture that surrounds us, then our formulation of the norm for faith and life will have to include a protest against the idolatry of this world.

At the same time we need to be mindful of the way religious forces subvert the gospel. Religion is too often its own worst enemy precisely because it takes so many oppressive forms, merging faith with the powers of this world. But some forms are dangerous precisely because they are so attractive to Americans. Here let me describe the strange mix which I call the American Cultural Religion. First, this cultural religion is *all about me*. The goals of personal growth and self-fulfillment are central. To achieve these, Christian faith is seen as something which one adds on to one's life to defend, expand or enhance personal interests and happiness. For middle class and upwardly mobile people, who have most of their physical and economic needs already met, add-on religion leaves every-thing in place but provides that missing piece of meaning, acceptance, or motivation to expand one's potential. Second, it gravitates toward the religion of power, rather than the religion of grace. That is, God will do more than love you, God will do things for you and empower you to do what you want. God exists to help us be healthy, strong, and successful.

Though it claims to focus on the Bible, too often its real authority is success in numbers and dollars. Third, this religion is highly individualistic. It relies on the American commitment to liberty and the pursuit of happiness rather than equality and community. It assumes that the individual is the principle of authority. The emergence of libertarianism among both liberals and conservatives attests to the way we value the freedom of the individual. Finally, this cultural religion endorses in an uncritical manner national, economic, and social values. It is quite willing to be the agent for blessing the status quo. This is made possible by embracing the long standing American claim to innocence. To preserve the current culture one must elevate it above all others and to do this one must engage in a rewriting of history which denies anything that threatens us.

Like Bunyan's faithful Pilgrim, we too are surrounded by dangers. On the one side are worldly forces, usually described as inevitable and necessary, such a globalization, the war on terror, or the survival of the fittest in the drive for success. On the other side is an indigenous cultural religion that turns everything into a means to enhance individual and/or cultural values. At times the two converge, as when religious people endorse excessive profits or wars. The attempt to reformulate the norm for faith and life today will have to be mindful of this cultural situation.

Given the concerns regarding the norm provided by Phillip Schaff and our new cultural situation, here is a revised norm for the church:

- The Formal Principle is Jesus Christ, the Word of God, affirmed in the Bible, tradition and creeds.

- The Material Principle is the new life in Christ, understood as gift and promise, with reference to the Gospels and Paul.

We begin with the Formal Principle in order to locate the source of faith and what shall be considered authoritative. There are, of course, other options such as the church and its traditions, or doctrines, or in a modern spirit, reason and the right of the individual to determine faith. But as this section and the following chapters will argue, we start instead with the confession of Jesus Christ as the Word of God. Such an affirmation moves in two directions: it is a theological statement about God; it is also a Christocentric statement directing our attention to Jesus of Nazareth and the salvation accomplished in him.

To frame the norm is this way calls the church to own its confession of God. The Word of God is the Word active in creation and the history of Israel. This God is the Almighty, the Creator of heaven and earth. God is the free sovereign who stands over against all worldly powers. To name this God is to confess that the world is not all there is, in spite of its claims to power, truth, and goodness. Since such claims are present in the church as well as the world, this norm affirms that the Word of God must first stand over against us before it can be for us. When Jesus announces the coming of the Kingdom of God, it is the rule of the Almighty, the Holy One of Israel.

If the intention is to signal that we must speak of God, just as surely we must speak of Jesus Christ. It is the story of the life, death, and resurrection of Jesus which has opened our eyes to what God is doing in the world. Therefore our faith and practice must be tested by Jesus Christ. To know him, however, requires attention to the witnesses to him: the New Testament, the creeds, and the growing traditions of faith and practice. Just as the field of discourse about God is given a specific focus when Jesus is designated the Word of God, so discourse about Jesus receives specific substance when we rely upon the witnesses to him found in the New Testament. Likewise, the norm insists that we interpret the Bible through the traditions of the church: the creeds, the development of faith and practice, the traditions of the Reformation as well as the great resources of ecumenical theology and biblical scholarship in the past century.

The Material principle uses the concept of new life to affirm the fullness of God's saving power in Jesus Christ. We need an inclusive category to affirm the magnitude of the redemption brought by Jesus Christ. New life gathers together justification and sanctification, the individual and the community, human life and the systems of nature, forgiveness and liberation from the powers of sin and death, this present time and the coming of the glory of God. New life witnesses to participation in a new spiritual reality, with heart, mind, and will. The image of life is used in the New Testament, the creeds, and the incarnational theology of the early church. It is reaffirmed in the theologies of John Williamson Nevin and Phillip Schaff, in fact, Schaff refers to his formulation of the material principle as the life principle.[3]

---

3. Ibid., 134–36, 154–55, 219–20, 228.

The norm declares that we must speak of the new life embodied in Jesus Christ. The culture considers new life in radically different ways: either it is already embedded in us, waiting to be released, or it is an entitlement, leading to success and worldly happiness. The former eliminates the need for repentance and new birth; the latter makes the goal something we deserve based on our achievements. By contrast, the norm leads us to discover that new life is found by losing oneself for the sake of Christ and God's Kingdom. John insists we must be born again into the spiritual unity of Christ, as branches are joined to the vine. Paul describes new life as participation in Jesus' death and resurrection. Taken together, these witnesses affirm that new life is tied to the new covenant sealed by Jesus' cross and resurrection. As Jesus is the Lord, so we are His people, the Body of Christ. The new life is not a confederation of solitary individuals, nor a contract between autonomous agents, but a union of those who confess that Jesus is Lord.

Finally, the new life in Christ is understood as gift and promise. As a gift, it is grounded in the grace of God and God's unchanging will to redeem the world. By our baptism we are marked by God and by our faith we receive all of Christ's blessings. We are named sons and daughters of God, freed from the power of sin and the fear of death. Because new life is a gift, we are united to one another not by our actions or agreement, but the will of God to create on earth the peace of Christ. Gifted by God, our identity is secure: it is God's new reality in Jesus Christ.

As a promise, new life is a pledge that Christ will be with us to the end of the age and that the Spirit will bestow gifts of love and joy, freedom and hope. Blessed with promise, we are called to see, to rely upon and to celebrate the glory of God now revealed in the world. We are therefore confessors who cannot keep silent but rejoice at the unfolding glory of God. Blessed with Christ's presence and the gifts of the Spirit, we seek to embody the love and peace of Christ. This, we believe, is the hope of the world.

The relation of the gift and promise is decisive for the way we define ourselves. Following Paul, we affirm that the only basis for life in Christ is God's gracious bestowal of righteousness received in faith. As a gift, our life in Christ means the end to all attempts to prove and defend ourselves, or to differentiate gradations of moral or spiritual status. We are called to live without claims regarding ourselves but only to claim God's grace.

The gift, however, contains within it the promise, which is our calling to discipleship.

Our failures to actualize this expectation do not mean that God takes back the gift. Rather they point to the tragic situation of our lives, where we still struggle with sin and the powers of this world. Conservatives have attempted to require new life by means of rules and regulations, playing upon guilt and the threat of exclusion. Liberals assume everyone knows what to do, need no rebirth, and have simply been distracted or made mistakes. But in desperation they too resort to rules, the use of guilt, and exclusion. Thus both conservatives and liberals would set requirements for the gift, based on their definition of the promise. Against such legalistic self-righteousness and naïve optimism, we confess that we are sinful yet justified by grace.

All of this means that we celebrate the gift and live in expectation of fulfilling the promise. We have done quite well at celebrating the gift, but have suffered drooping hands and weak knees regarding God's expectations. As Protestants, our challenge is to join our moral realism with a more bold eschatological hope. That is, we readily confess that we are still bound to the alienation and strife of this world. We lament that we do not fully participate in the Rule of God. We consider this to be part of the sorrow of this world. But can we turn with equal rigor to conforming to the mind of Christ—without falling prey to utopian dreams or legalistic structures. Since our identity is in the gift, we dare not despair. The gift and the promise cause us to have hope and take heart, as we again and again look to the revealing of God's glory now and forevermore. The gift makes it possible for us to live with every expectation of the promises of God.

This then is the norm proposed for our definition of the church. The explanation given here is brief, since further rationale and interpretation will be given as we proceed through the other five essential components of the definition of the church.

three

Authority

The Third Essential Component:

The church is a community which affirms the authority of God in Christ and claims authority from Christ for its life and work.

The Formation of Centers of Authority

IN THEORY AND IN fact we know that a new community must have a principle of authority to justify its existence and guide its life. The early church, however, did not have a constitutional convention to settle once and for all the issues of authority. Nor did it move directly from the risen Lord to a completed structure governed by St. Peter. Rather, the church was formed over centuries—and is still in the process of being formed and reformed.[1] As one looks at this development of the church, two things catch our attention. One is that there are multiple centers of authority. Their emergence is tied to the specific needs and challenges of times and places. This reveals the freedom and creativity of churches as they seek to be faithful in new times. The second is that given multiple forms of

---

1. For readers unfamiliar with the history of the church during the first five centuries, it would be helpful to consult with one of the readily available, standard works: for example, the revised edition of Williston Walker's basic work or the more recent history by Justo L. Gonzalez. Cf. Walker et al., *History of the Christian Church*; Gonzalez, *The Story of Christianity*.

authority, each having a specific history, there will be competition and even tension between them. We may quickly illustrate both points.

From what has been said about the church as a new creation by God in Christ, it is obvious that the primary authority was Jesus Christ—his teachings and actions, as well as his crucifixion and resurrection. For this reason, those who had actually known Jesus, who were called and commissioned by him, were recognized to provide leadership and determine valid testimony regarding Jesus. This constitutes the first great change in authority: the transmission of authority from Jesus to the apostles. The apostles have authority as witnesses and guardians of the faith because of their relation to Jesus. Two examples illustrate how important apostolic authority was for the early church: one is the need to connect each of the four Gospels with one of the disciples, thereby confirming its reliability; another is Paul's justification of his teaching by reference to his call by Christ to be an apostle, even though he was not part of the original twelve disciples.

The second great change came with the death of all of the apostles. But this transition to the second generation did not occur all at once. Even when the apostles were alive, there were churches without direct supervision by an apostle. Thus the oral and written traditions connected to the apostles already functioned with authority while they were alive. When the transition to the second generation was complete, these traditions of the apostles continued to guide churches, thus becoming a different form of authority. Moreover, these traditions quickly expanded over time in response to the needs of growing congregations. Once the Christian community includes both Jewish and Gentile Christians, in Palestine and throughout the Roman world, congregations face innumerable challenges. Imagine the difference between trying to tell the story of Jesus to a Jew (already a monotheist who knows Hebrew Scriptures) and a Gentile (probably a polytheist with absolutely no knowledge of the traditions of Abraham, Moses, and David). In simple terms, the tradition grows in order to meet pressing needs: within the congregations they needed to set standards for worship, teaching children and converts, as well as practices for daily life; as congregations in the Roman empire, they were faced with questions of their relation to Roman rule and had to determine what religious, moral, and social practices are acceptable. Consider one of the longest and most influential writings in the second century by Irenaeus in southern France: in great detail he describes the religious views of Hellenistic religions which, if adopted, would completely destroy the message of Jesus.[2] His readers were not bothered at all by the prospect of believing in God; what they could not understand was why they should believe in *only one God.*

All of this suggests a very dynamic process, where traditions develop in relation to internal needs and the challenges of the external culture. But note that beside things directly associated with the apostles, we now find new leaders, an expanding apostolic tradition, along with practices regarding worship and community life. Add to these centers of authority a list of decisions, made in the midst of controversy. From the apostles' decision to include Gentiles, to the second-century decision against Marcion, and numerous judgments which shall follow, the church is given form and substance by great decisions.[3] It is on the basis of such developments within the early church that it is possible to speak of *multiple centers of authority.* That these forms of authority develop and have a history, that they vary from fixed documents to practices subject to variation, or that they provide standards and yet create problems—all these things give us insight into the nature of authority in Christian communities. Consider then these six centers of authority:

1. *Practices of the community* over time, come to be a part of the apostolic tradition. These practices relate to worship and the celebration of baptism and the Eucharist, evangelism, the exercise of leadership, the internal life of the community as well as its relation to the world. A good example of how practices can become authoritative while still leaving room for change and variety is the liturgies for the Eucharist. While it is possible to identity the essential elements of the liturgy honored by centuries of use, there is still a great difference between our worship services and those of the first four centuries. Thus we are faced with the paradoxical claim that our particular liturgies are faithful to the tradition, even though they are quite differ-

2. Cf. Irenaeus, "Against Heresies," 309–567.

3. Marcion was a second-century Christian whose views were rejected because, among other things, he tried to solve the problem of evil by suggesting two gods—one good and the other evil. See the later reference in this chapter. Cf. Walker, *A History,* 67–69.

ent from anything in the early church. The fact is practices develop and change, yet still possess authority.

2. Closely related to practices are the *leaders* who must guide churches in light of the apostolic witness. The New Testament refers to several kinds of leaders in the early church: those with oversight (the Greek word is *episcope*), presbyters or priests and deacons. It is clear that at a very early stage the churches recognized the need to create leadership roles and to invest them with levels of authority. In the initial period, however, these roles were quite fluid and did not possess all the meaning they have today.[4]

3. *Written documents* emerged in the first generation of Christians, the first being letters and compilations of sayings of Jesus. These were followed by the Gospels. Before the church established a canon (i.e., standard) of sacred writings like the Hebrew Scriptures, other writings appeared and some even competed for inclusion in what came to be the New Testament. Some writings circulated widely among Christians and exercised great influence, even though they never were considered canonical. For example, the already mentioned work of Irenaeus, *Against Heresies*, or the popular work by Athanasius on the life of St. Anthony.[5] Once a collection of writings reached the level of Sacred Scripture, it came to possess pre-eminent authority because it was seen as the witness of the apostles to the life, death, and resurrection of Jesus.[6]

4. *Short confessions* of faith stated what the churches believed and also set limits for faith, used in teaching, worship, and evangelism. We see some of these in the sermons in the Book of Acts and in Paul's letters. In time they came to present a simple summary of what Christians believe. They were called creeds, since they begin with the Latin word *credo*, or I believe. The earliest reference to the Apostles' Creed is in the second century.[7] Its very name illustrates the importance of connecting faith to the first followers of Jesus. The Nicene Creed and the Definition of Chalcedon emerged from three councils between

4. Cf. . Gonzalez, *The Story*, 97ff. and Walker, *A History*, 45–49.
5. Cf. Gonzalez, *The Story*, 138ff.
6. Ibid., 62–66 and Walker, *A History*, 71–75.
7. Cf. Leith, *Creeds of the Churches*, 20–36.

325 to 451, dealing with issues regarding God and Jesus Christ. In theory, creeds are supposed to resolve issues and establish the limits for faith, but that is not always the case. Some Protestants claim to be non-creedal traditions, claiming only the Bible, or some brief statement regarding Jesus Christ. What is seldom discussed is that even in this revised or downsized version, these churches function with the equivalent of a creed.

5. *Landmark decisions* resolve a serious debate or conflict in the life of the church. These decisions may be less known to the average Christian than the other four elements. They are treated separately here for several reasons.

First, some of the decisions are only indirectly tied to creeds. It is also the case that today many can recite certain creeds but have no idea what problem or decision inspired the creed. Thus for many people the Nicene Creed is an answer without a question.

Second, these decisions have had tremendous formative power in shaping the faith and life of the church. If, for example, the churches had followed the view of Marcion in the second century, they would be cut off from the Hebrew Bible with a New Testament consisting of Luke and the Pauline letters.[8] Creation would be separated from redemption, each the work of a different deity. A similar argument can be made for other decisions. If one looks at them over the first five centuries, one sees a string of great decisions which shaped the apostolic tradition. Once made, these decisions—at least in theory—do not have to be re-argued and come to have authority for future generations. However, in some cases, a landmark decision is debated again in every generation (e.g., the debate between Augustine and Pelagius over the magnitude of sin).

Finally, landmark decisions deserve attention because they illustrate the nature of authority in the church. If the source of all authority is God's act in Christ, then faithful witnesses to that event are endowed with authority from God. Just consider, for example, how many times people have used one of Paul's landmark decisions in teaching or sermons. To this day a strange church debate over meat blessed in pagan rituals is still recalled as a source of guidance. Of

8. Cf. Conzalez, *The Story,* 61–62.

course, Paul's insistence regarding the inclusion of Gentiles into the Christian community, without first having to become Jews, led to an even greater decision. Landmark decisions arise out of unpredictable crises and churches are forced to make decisions. Could the church make wrong decisions? Of course. Could a decision be so tied to a time and place that it needed to be revised at a later time? Quite possibly, and indeed, it has happened many times.

6. A final entry to this list is the authority of *culture*.[9] Since a community of faith is always in a specific context, culture provides form and structure. Some of these structures or limits are neutral, in and of themselves: e.g., language, geography, climate, and access to natural resources. Others are more complicated: e.g., social, economic, and political traditions. To say these have no effect upon faith and practice would deny that the church is always embedded in particular cultures. For example, governments expect citizens to be loyal, participate in military service, and pay taxes. In a quite different way, major scientific and technological discoveries create problems for faith and life. For example, the Copernican revolution changed the way we think about the world and forced the church to maintain or revise the biblical cosmology. In the current debates over worship, one frequently hears that we need to change things because people are less auditory and more visual in the way they communicate. Whether this is true or not, note the appeal to the power of culture to determine an outcome. In all of these examples, culture exercises varying degrees of influence and control over the churches. In turn, churches react to these interventions in a wide range of ways and this becomes a major point of division.[10]

In reviewing this list of centers of authority, several categories are absent. There is no mention of reason, experience, or conscience. Some traditions, such as the United Methodist, have included reason and ex-

9. I am indebted to my colleague Lee Barrett for the suggestion to include culture as a center of authority. For most it is an implied force in setting limits or requiring changes, but seldom is it officially recognized as an authority along with such things like Scripture or tradition. The United Methodist fourfold standard includes reason and experience, which open the door to culture.

10. Cf. the influential study by H. Richard Niebuhr on the ways Christians interact with culture: *Christ and Culture*.

perience in the famous fourfold set of standards, along with Scripture and tradition. By their inclusion we are reminded that the future always presents issues not addressed by Scripture and tradition. In the modern age, individual conscience has taken on a certain sanctity as a symbol of the courageous individual standing against tyrannical authority. The three concepts (i.e., reason, experience, and conscience) are not included in this list because they are so open-ended and lack specific meaning. One is forced to ask: what norm is one using to reason, to evaluate experience, or guide conscience. There are so many times when appeals to reason, experience and conscience mislead people that they do not, by themselves suggest standards for faith. For example, Pelagius—and his followers to this day—insisted that reason justified his position against that of Augustine. Put in another way, there is no independent reason, experience, or conscience. We reason from within faith and/or a set of values. New experiences are evaluated and assimilated into the larger experience of the individual and community. Some might respond that reason should be included as an authority in order to emphasize truth as a standard for faith. But the concern for truth is already contained in the six centers of authority. Reason as the quest for truth does not act independently of community practices, governing decisions or even Scripture, but is a part of the lively debate always going on within the community as it uses the six centers of authority.

Centers of Authority in Conflict

When one steps back from this list of centers of authority, great questions emerge:

- Which of the six centers of authority is primary?
- Who has authority to interpret Scripture.
- What do we do when Scripture appears to contradict itself?
- What if traditional practices or bishops appear to diverge from the creeds or Scripture?
- What do we do when faced with issues not covered by the first five sources of authority?
- On what basis do we accept changes in the culture?

These questions reveal how multiple sources of authority create continuous discussion, debate, and conflict. When one adds in the factors of different times and places, new opportunities and dangers, one is faced with a very open-ended and dynamic process. Consider the way Luther uses the authority of Scripture to challenge bishops and traditions of the church. But this was not the first time for such conflict. The struggle between the bishops and the teachers of the church was perennial, especially if one includes in the teaching office the monastic movements, which were critical of contemporary church life. But we hardly need to refer to the past to illustrate how the six centers of authority may conflict. The current debates over human rights, women's rights, sexual orientation, war and peace, the environment, and economic issues illustrate the same complexity. In one sense, the alienation of Roman Catholic laity from the church hierarchy over child abuse represents a protest against the abuse of power in the name of traditional moral standards.

Churches may be distinguished by the way they organize these centers of authority and thereby resolve many of the tensions. The Roman Catholic tradition gives priority to the bishops and traditions of the church (i.e., theology and practice). The fact that both Scripture and creeds came out of the church allows it to argue that these documents need to be interpreted by the bishops and traditions of the church. From this point of view, conflicts within Scripture or between Scripture and contemporary practice are resolved by the church leaders. Likewise, it is acceptable for practices to develop over many centuries that are not in the New Testament (e.g., monastic movements, a celibate clergy, and seven sacraments). Yet there has always been tension within the Roman tradition over two issues: one is the tension between the bishops and the teachers of the church; the other is the tension between all the bishops (represented by the councils) and the bishop of Rome. In theory these issues were resolved in the nineteenth century with the doctrine of the infallibility of the Pope, though one still finds opposition to this concentration of authority in one part of the church.

The Eastern Orthodox traditions share the Roman Catholic preference for the authority of bishops, traditions and creeds, though these groups never accepted the authority of the bishop of Rome. They are also distinctive in their reliance on the theology of the first five centuries, which produced the ecumenical creeds, and of course the rich liturgical traditions of sacraments, music, and icons. Since these churches were somewhat protected from the western European crises of the Renaissance, Reformation, and Enlightenment, they are tied to the ancient traditions far more than Roman Catholics and Protestants. But the global communication of the past half-century is creating changes.

The Protestant movements arose over objections to specific practices and abuses, as well as a bold affirmation of certain themes from the New Testament. When confronted with opposition from the bishops and long-standing traditions, Luther appealed to the authority of Scripture as over-ruling the bishops and traditional practices. Having framed the debate in this way, it was inevitable that Luther would be excommunicated. But this only highlighted the confidence Luther had in claiming the authority of Scripture as the final authority. Since the church was now defined in terms of the witness of Scripture, rather than the witness of bishops and questionable traditions, being excommunicated did not remove the protestors from what they affirmed as the true church. Thus arose the distinctive Protestant slogan of the primacy of Scripture (*sola scriptura*).

Things got more complicated when Luther was confronted by other reform movements that also appealed to Scripture, but differed from Luther over such things as infant baptism. In such debates Luther had to make clear that all along he took the New Testament themes of the sovereignty of God and the primacy of grace to be the keys to Scripture. Moreover, when faced with the charge that he was claiming the right of the individual to disagree with the authority of bishops and traditions, Luther and his followers were quick to admit that they interpreted the New Testament through the writings of St. Augustine and the ecumenical creeds. This defense of Luther's position, however, opened the door for many other Protestants to argue that they too claimed Scripture to be primary, but read it from a different perspective. So we find some taking the Sermon on the Mount and Matthew 18 as the center of Scripture, while others looked to Pentecost, the bestowal of the Spirit, or the transformation to holiness as the key. Millennial expectations have dominated many new traditions during the past two hundred years. From the Roman Catholic perspective, this proliferation of Protestant groups only confirms its conviction that without the guidance of the bishops and tradition, there will be any number of groups claiming authority for different beliefs and practices.

To explore how these centers of authority function in the life of the church—and in relation to one another—several specific issues shall be examined.

The Authority of Scripture

In the current situation in America, there have been major changes in the way traditions interpret Scripture. Biblical studies among Roman Catholics and Protestants have created common ground in spite of traditional doctrinal differences. One finds continual ferment among conservative Protestants as new generations find the traditional affirmation of an inerrant Bible, inspired word for word, to be problematic. And there have been surprising developments among mainline Protestants. In this new situation four approaches to the authority of the Bible have emerged:

The first is the affirmation that the Bible is inerrant, inspired word for word, and is the sole authority for believers. The advantage of this approach is that it sees the Bible as the self-evident Word of God and the sole authority for believers. The burden of this view is that adherents must spend considerable time fighting an uphill battle defending against criticisms from within and outside the faith.

The second approach affirms that the Bible is the faithful witness to God's salvation revealed in Israel and Jesus Christ. As such it is inspired by God and is the primary authority for faith. But it is the Word of God for us only through the inspiration of the Holy Spirit; without the Spirit it is words printed on pages. The advantage of this view is that it retains the primacy of Scripture but avoids all the problems connected to contradictions within the Bible, as well as conflicts with modern science and political and social practices. The challenge here, however, is to gain agreement on the substance of the witness.

The third approach affirms that the Bible is authoritative but must be interpreted by the church in light of creeds, theology, and practices. This view is traditionally associated with Roman Catholics. But further support for this approach comes, somewhat surprisingly, from two other sources: one is the history of biblical study, which argues that the Bible must be interpreted in light of its literary and historical origin; the second consists of theories of interpretation which insist that every text is understood not simply by what words are on the page but by the linguistic and cultural values readers bring to the text. From quite different perspectives, both of these traditions argue that the Bible is not self-evident but needs to be interpreted.

The fourth view initially appears to be a bold departure from the other three. It holds that the Bible has no authority unless it agrees with the values of the reader and/or a community of faith. Instead of claiming some kind of neutrality, proponents of this view willingly state that they bring to the Bible the standards for deciding its value. When this view appears among some feminist writers, it means that they start with a commitment to equality and justice for women. They will not accept any Scripture passage that contradicts these values. In a similar way, black theologians have argued that the liberation of black people is the standard for reading the Bible.

Reduced to their simplest form, we have four distinctive approaches to Scripture. One can also track them through the past five hundred years as they appear in the great conflicts between Roman Catholics and Protestants, and between Protestants themselves. But in the past several generations, the four approaches have become quite fluid, with movement in all directions. Consider the following:

As mainline Protestants become more willing to affirm that they read Scripture with theological traditions, creeds, and the newspaper, it becomes more difficult to affirm that Scripture is the *only* authority (i.e., *sola Scriptura*). If one adds to this the current emphasis on how texts require communities of interpretation, one soon finds traditional Protestants sounding like Roman Catholics.

As more conservative Protestants find it impossible or unnecessary to argue about the correctness of every verse, or how every verse has equal authority, one finds movement away from traditional literalism. This could mean adopting the view that the Bible is the authoritative witness to Christ, or accepting the assistance of the community in interpreting the text.

The fourth approach differs from the other three by not starting with some declaration of the Bible's authority independent of us. It prompts the charge that the reader is setting up a prior source of authority outside of Scripture. Criticisms of arrogance and rebelliousness soon follow. But is this view really that different from the third approach, which for centuries has said that the Bible must be read according to the values and belief systems of the Christian community? Likewise, many conservative and liberal Protestants can be found saying that a particular passage of Scripture need not be binding because it conflicts with current knowledge or values. For example, consider their attitude toward the age of the earth as four to five thousand years, polygamy, divorce, slavery, monarchy, and the silence of women in church. It would appear that the feminist appeal to the value of equality is not that different from an orthodox Calvinist saying he sides with modern science over the biblical cosmology. What we have then, is that in our situation, those so comfortable in assuming that they did not impose anything on the Bible must now recognize that they, like everyone else, brings values to their reading of the Bible.

These shifting positions mean that we live in a time when the traditional options for defining the authority of the Bible are under reconsideration and several positions are moving closer to one another. While this can be confusing, since it is hard to identify the current positions using the older labels, it is also encouraging. Underlying the shifting positions is a recognition that the authority of the Bible is far more complex than what one might have imagined. The former options of either/or are being replaced by more subtle combinations that are not easily defined by the older slogans.

The Multiple Relations of Church and Culture

I have suggested that culture interacts with the church in numerous ways: it provides a context in which churches exist, it places requirements upon the church and may also challenge the church in positive and negative ways. As a consequence, there is no single way to describe the relation of the church to culture. In fact, the interactions are often quite paradoxical, involving great tension and resistance as well as a reaffirmation of values inherent in the tradition. Take for example, the abolition of slavery and equal rights for women. On the one hand, both struggles involved long standing traditions supporting slavery and subordination of women. The resistance to these movements toward freedom was too often based on appeals to theology and Scripture. On the other hand, the quest for freedom could be supported by the same Bible and communal practices such as baptism and Eucharist. At major stages of the movements for freedom over the past 200 years, churches repented of their former practices. In some cases this was because of the power of social and political values in the culture; in other cases it was because of what was already in churches' collective memory, namely, that Jesus means equality at the Lord's Table. What we have, then, is not a simple relation of culture to churches but a quite complex one. At times culture appears as launching an assault on revered practices, yet for many the liberation of African Americans and women has led to a more faithful form of the church.

A quite different dynamic seems to be at work in the great struggle over the Copernican revolution. In this case, the challenge comes from outside the Bible and church tradition, based on claims to reason and scientific method. There was no easy resolution of the opposing world views. In this sense, the scientific discoveries do stand outside of the known world of Christian thought and practice and possess an authority of their own, forcing a response from churches. What is of interest at this point is why and how churches accepted the new world view (of course, in different stages). One can argue that the new world view became acceptable because it could be assimilated into the reason and experience of the community. If people were actually circumnavigating the earth, the biblical map of the world and the three-story universe no longer appeared to be a truthful way of describing God's creation. But the result was not simply the acceptance of an idea formulated by reason outside of faith, but a new way of thinking about God's creation in light of Copernicus' worldview. The paradox of this becomes illustrated in the music of Joseph Haydn: *The Creation*. For the eighteenth century, the new cosmology only made the heavens a more wonderful revelation of the glory of God.

If this type of analysis is correct, we have a different way of understanding the interactions between church and culture. Culture can indeed challenge the church but these challenges can also be the occasion for recovery of its own values. Other occasions involve challenges that do indeed require a revision of a traditional article of faith, as with the doctrine of creation. In all three cases, there is loss and gain: On the one hand they represent a crisis because old ideas and practices are challenged; on the other hand the revisions are facilitated by connections between the new and the old. To risk a contemporary example, the inclusion of homosexuals into the community represents both loss and gain. There is the crisis of having to set aside a way of thinking and practice. But there is the gain of a new awareness that the peace of Christ is at work among us, affirming all of God's people. In the face of the challenge of this issue, some find the old practices of violence, hate, and exclusion to be contrary to the love of Christ. Traditional practice is overruled by the need to be reconciled, even with those who are radically different. In other words, some are ultimately persuaded not by new information or new doctrine, but they are constrained by God's will to unite us in Christ.

The Domination of Culture

The faith and practice of churches are sorely tested when culture intrudes to the point of domination. Here we need to consider several examples where culture frames the issues for the churches, or intrudes so forcefully that culture dominates the church's values. Instead of being in positive interaction with the other centers of authority, it overrules them.

Consider the way the culture imposes on the church the polarity of the Left and Right in American culture. There was a time when liberal and conservative positions were fairly easy to track, with key words like freedom and order symbolizing the two perspectives. But in the past fifty years the rival positions have become so complicated that each position is hard to define. James Davison Hunter proposed that we think of the opposition between left and right as a *culture war*, extending over time, involving multiple issues.[11] This proposal was helpful in reminding us of the duration of the struggle and how old wounds still had the power to arouse feelings. Likewise, it allows us to see the carry over from one issue to another: both sides found that they opposed one another on many issues. This made it difficult to find a common ground where people could come together in addressing a new issue. The mistrust was cumulative and only intensified because so many issues divided the two sides.

Hunter proposed that the primary source of division was opposing views of authority.[12] If conservatives saw authority as fixed, providing an unchangeable source of guidance in a changing world, liberals were more likely to be open to new knowledge, allowing traditional values to be revised in light of new experience. There is no doubt that different views of authority go to the heart of the liberal-conservative divide. What was given less attention in this analysis, however, was the way other key con-

11. Cf. James Davison Hunter, *Culture Wars: The Struggle to Define America*.
12. Ibid., 68–128.

cepts generated polarization. These functioned with such force that one could argue that they exercised authority for the two communities. What are these concepts?

- One is the way each side thinks about freedom: conservatives tend to see freedom as the ability to conform to traditional social standards, whereas liberals see freedom in terms of self-actualization. If the former fear rebellion leading to chaos, the latter fear social pressures that restrict or repress the individual.

- A second is different views of sin: conservatives tend to see sin as violation of rules and social standards regarding personal life, giving less attention to broad political, social, or economic practices; liberals tend to see sin as repressive acts by society against individuals or the environment, playing down individual rebellion or self-centeredness. With regard to individuals, liberals tend to show concern for self-imposed limitations and the refusal to grow toward maturity, but are reluctant to draw conclusions that might minimize their optimism regarding human nature. In a break with orthodoxy, both sides are reluctant to speak of sin as the corruption of mind, heart, and will. Conservatives sound like they hold individuals responsible, but too often blame the devil; liberals are willing to speak of immoral social forces, but are reluctant to connect them with individuals, except for individuals being victims.

- Finally, if conservatives see salvation in individual terms (forgiveness, abundant life, the assurance of life in heaven), liberals see salvation as self-actualization, freedom from oppressive forces, and the mature life on earth.

When one examines this polarization between liberals and conservatives, questions need to be addressed to both sides:

- On what authority does one determine that freedom must conform to social norms that are historically repressive of people of color and women, or that freedom is the individual's drive for self-actualization?

- On what authority does one conclude that sin does not pertain to social exploitation or individual self-centeredness, or even the corruptibility of all things?

- On what authority does one conclude that salvation only confers benefits on the individual on earth, or in heaven, or only liberation from social forces?

Such questions suggest that both liberals and conservatives have allowed the culture to frame the discussion and dominate their basic values. This subordinates the Christian tradition to the dominant cultural values. It is very hard to find in Scripture, creed, or theology the justification for the kind of extremes defended in the culture war. This raises the fundamental question: if the church is to reclaim its own authority for faith and practice, can it separate itself from the ritual warfare of Left and Right?

Other examples of the power of cultural values to dominate faith and practice are readily at hand: one is *autonomy* and the other is the *American way of life*. Most Americans place greater emphasis on liberty than justice or equality. But in the present scene liberty means quite different things. This is because the passion for liberty grows in direct proportion to what issue is being discussed. One can become a libertarian by moving from a liberal position in search of individual freedom in the face of a repressive society, or by moving from a conservative position in search of political and economic freedom in the face of government regulation. In both cases, the individual is considered the basic unit of social order and the maximization of individual rights is seen as the goal. In the case of liberals, this quest for freedom means freedom from a repressive society and restrictions on sexual practice, speech or artistic expression. In the case of conservatives, the quest for freedom means freedom from government controls as well as laws protecting abortion, gay rights, civil rights, and federal welfare programs.

The cultural norm of autonomy has made serious inroads into religious life. Much of popular religion prides itself on being independent of national denominations. Most of the church growth success stories are independent churches—reluctant even to use traditional labels like Baptist. To be independent is proclaimed as a mark of distinction: to be a local church not bound in any way by ties to regional and national bodies. (Could there be a bolder denial of unity and catholicity?) On one trip through western Pennsylvania I passed a church sign: "Independent Fellowship." I doubt if they saw the humor or the contradiction in that nameplate.

The quest for autonomy is not only among the conservative, free church branches of the faith. The United Church of Christ, created in 1957, celebrated the unity in Christ of diverse traditions. At the same time the founders inserted into the Constitution and By-laws the principle of autonomy. Every part of the church—national, regional, and local—is autonomous. This policy can be traced back to the struggle of Congregational churches in the seventeenth century to be free from the state church and bishops in England. But such freedom was transformed into the nineteenth- and twentieth-century principle of autonomy, a value that cannot be found in the New Testament or the Reformers. Since it is written into the Constitution and By-laws, it even takes precedence over appeals to Scripture and tradition. Equally disturbing is the general sense that other Lutheran and Reformed communities are also dominated by the idea of the freedom of individuals and congregations from communal structures.

If churches mimic the culture in adoration of autonomy, the same can be said regarding the churches' defense of the American Way of Life. The goals of health, wealth, and prosperity dominate public religion in America, where God is perceived as the defender of our way of life. For example, no matter how many times it is admitted by liberals and conservatives that our foreign policies (and wars) in the Middle East are tied to unlimited oil consumption, neither the churches nor the general public demand a change. The problem is that change would require a change in the way we live our lives. In the 2010 British Petroleum oil spill in the Gulf of Mexico, the lack of regulation was again an issue. Yet it is difficult to rally support for tighter safety controls and greater protection of the environment. In fact, even in the face of this disaster many clamor for less government regulation, no matter what the costs. When one considers traditional Christian thought, whether it is rooted in St. Augustine or Calvin, it is difficult to justify the absence of regulation. We again are confronted with the fact that the culture has cut the churches off from their unique sources of authority.

There is another way in which contemporary culture weakens the church's claim to authority. When religious traditions are marginalized and considered personal preferences, it is inevitable that a loss of conviction occurs regarding traditional sources of authority. A pragmatic and secular culture has neither time nor respect for appeals to religion.

Stephen Carter argued forcefully in *The Culture of Disbelief* that American culture has reduced all religious claims to individual choices. Lacking any objective verification for Christian claims, such claims are reduced to subjective preferences, not relevant in public discourse. Moreover, it is best to keep religion in the private sector, since religion is a source of division. Insisting that someone consider a religious claim is like insisting that your preferences regarding music could be binding on another person.[13]

Carter's concern needs to be taken seriously, since mainline Protestantism suffers not from being too liberal but from lack of conviction regarding its own commitments. One can hold to liberal, ecumenical religious convictions without being obnoxious or oppressive. But somehow in the past generation, we see an erosion of conviction. This in turn takes us back to our core Christological convictions. If believing that Jesus Christ is Lord is reduced to a personal preference, which is rude to mention in polite conversation, it is not surprising that all centers of authority are diminished. If the Christological core is uncertain, why should certain practices, Scripture, creed, or the moral authority of the church be honored?

The Church's Claim to Authority

The Paradox of Authority

One might well ask why Christianity has such a complex and controversial structure of authority. Why not a simple answer to simple questions, with clear lines of absolute authority? To be sure, some would quickly say this is what should be affirmed. But this usually entails a retreat into some form of a mighty fortress, claiming absolute authority. I would prefer moving in a quite different direction. The answer to these questions lies in the origin of the church and the general development of the church described thus far. There is an absolute authority and it is God and only God. But God invests things of this world with authority to speak and act in the name of God. The disciples are called and commissioned as apostles, yet authority is entrusted to them only as witnesses to Jesus Christ. They do not have authority by virtue of their own power or achievement. Neither do they have authority to change the message nor authority to do harm to anyone.

13. Cf. Stephen Carter, *The Culture of Disbelief.*

Their authority is derived from Christ and they embody this authority only in their fidelity to him. They do not take the place of Christ, but represent him to the world. In this sense, anyone who represents Christ to the world, as did the women who witnessed to the resurrection, possess authority from Christ. Christ's authority is not confined by time, space, or office. Authority is a gift of the Spirit and cannot be controlled by human desire or design. It is real and invested in particular people and actions, but it is never absolute. It has its power only as it reflects the light of Christ.[14]

All of this is to say that authority must be understood in a dynamic and paradoxical way: it is in this world but may not be completely equated with a practice, a text, or a person. To borrow a phrase from Paul, we have this treasure in earthen vessels. There are centers of authority for the church—time honored practices, bishops and pastors, Scripture, creeds, landmark decisions, and even aspects of culture. But no one of these is a sacred object; none reveals God in a self-evident way. None can be made into an absolute because only God is God and the church lives amid the changes of this world, still struggling with sin and grace.

The limits of churchly authority are derived from more than one source. In part they are established by the difference between God the Creator and the finite creation. The commandments against graven images and against taking the name of the Lord God in vain point in this direction. There is a difference between God and the world which cannot be forgotten. God is sovereign and free, and this freedom means that God cannot be controlled or encapsulated. But the limits of the church's authority also stem from the continuing presence of sin among the faithful. The church's practices, theology, and decisions are not simply limited; they also bear the marks of self-interest and ill will. To the extent that the centers of authority perpetuate the divisions among people, protect special interests and privilege, fail to be self-critical, at those points we see the marks of our fallen humanity. Finally, the limits stem from the passage of time and changes in place. How wonderful it would be if one could overcome the limits of time and space, with pronouncements free of all of the ambiguity of language, culture, gender, and race. But such wisdom

14. This point is made in a dramatic way in Ignazio Silone's *Bread and Wine*. In the face of the church's collaboration with Mussolini's dictatorship in Italy, a revolutionary disguises himself as a priest. He goes about speaking the truth and bestowing kindness to those in need. So who are the true priests: the official ones supporting the government or the unofficial one who does what priests ought to do?

and power are not given to us—unless we overreach and pretend that we are gods.

A writer who saw the dilemma of claiming authority, understood in this paradoxical way, was H. Richard Niebuhr. In *The Kingdom of God in America*, Niebuhr posed the problem as the tension between affirming faith in the sovereign God, who stands in judgment of all things in this world, while at the same time needing to claim the importance of a particular act, text, or event in the church's life.[15] To put it in simple terms, how does a pastor tell the congregation that it is crucial to be at an event, when at the same time she knows that our frail systems may not dare to claim absolute importance. Just being aware of the paradox is enough to strike fear in the heart. The only way congregations can survive is to have a sense of confidence that the many practices are worth doing; and the only way congregations can faithfully survive is to know that all their practices are not absolute, but things done in faith and love as offerings to God. But it is knowing this that makes all the difference. St. Paul's words may be appropriate: "work out your own salvation with fear and trembling . . ." (Phil 2:12). The risk of overstating the church's authority should not prevent us from affirming that the church has authority. The new creation of the church is both gift and promise: the gift of new life which authorizes the community; the promise of continued life until the end of time.

Not all Christians agree with this view of authority. Many find it intolerable that we do not affirm an absolute point of authority. Given the madness of this world, where every imaginable thing has become a reality, there is obviously a great longing for the certainty derived from absolute authority. In the course of church history, we can see three mighty fortresses, erected as bulwarks against the storms of this world. One is the absolute authority of the church, another is the affirmation of an absolute and inerrant Bible, and the third is the reliance on an absolute and final set of doctrines. In each case, the claim to authority has been magnified to the point of perfection and infallibility. But at what cost? In the case of the absolute church—be it Roman Catholic or conservative Protestant—the claim is made for infallibility when the record simply will not support such a claim. The persistence of such claims for the church only tends to generate a large number of refugees, alienated from these churches and religion itself. In the case of the absolute Bible, the claim is made that this

15. Cf. Niebuhr, *The Kingdom of God in America*.

written document transcends its origin in the specifics of time and place, possessing absolute authority. This attempt to find a secure starting point for faith, however, only forces the Bible to bear more authority than was intended. Believers are forced into endless attempts to explain and justify all manner of things indirectly related to its basic message. Instead of finding its authority in the trustworthy witness to God's presence among us, we are instead diverted into debates which only detract from our witness to God. The same concerns must be raised against those who would make doctrines the absolute authority for faith and life. The creeds and great theological writings were intended to witness to God, not capture God in words on a page. They are invaluable guides and support against many of the challenges from inside and outside the church. But something goes wrong when documents of the past are taken out of their context and made absolute. Then they no longer serve as witnesses to God but become fences which confine minds and hearts. By restricting the freedom of faith they run the risk of destroying it.

Claiming the authority of Christ

The challenge facing the church is to recognize the authority contained in the new life in Christ and to claim it for the governance of the community. From the standpoint of Christian faith, God's will is not hidden but made known in the redemption of Israel and the unfolding redemption of the world through Jesus Christ. The authority given to the church is not the authority to have power over others (as James and John requested), nor the authority of status above others. Rather the authority of the church lies in the new life given to it: to be in this world as a representation of the reconciliation between God and humanity; to be the embodiment of the peace of Christ in a violent world; to witness to the God who is from all time self-giving and drawing the world into the divine love.

Claiming this authority is a challenge because of the fear and suspicion regarding all authority. In this world authority is used for personal gain and the protection of vested interests. It has been used to justify every manner of violence against the weak and poor. As a consequence, many are suspicious of power and fear its abuse. The practices of slavery and segregation, or the subordination of women, were all legal and condoned by the authority of churches. To this day the Mennonite character is formed by the remembrance of the persecution of their martyrs at the hands of all of the state churches. Mainline churches presently receive a significant number of new members who are refugees from the authoritarian structures of other branches of the church. In such a world, claiming authority goes against the grain of many church cultures which are trying to avoid being dogmatic and authoritarian.

How then is it possible to claim authority today? Let us begin by ruling out the options which are antithetical to the gospel. The problem we face is not a public relations or marketing problem. Nor is it, in the broad sense, a matter of strategic planning or leadership training. Learning new leadership techniques and planning strategies, while helpful in specific situations, are not the primary answer. To be sure, many claim authority because the promise of health, wealth, or a positive outlook proves to draw listeners and money. But these are short lived and basically peripheral to the issues facing most churches. Above all, claiming authority will not take place by trying to rival the three mighty fortresses mentioned above. All three absolute claims—for the church, Scripture, and doctrine—represent at the most fundamental level a claim to power. The absolute church rules over people and suppresses their voices. The claim to possess an infallible book or a compendium of absolute doctrine may give assurance to some, but for too many these mean the end to genuine inquiry and dialogue. For too long these three claims have used guilt or the fear of exclusion to control the faithful. But we are living at a time when these forms of power will control fewer and fewer of the faithful.

The real answer is already before us: the only way to claim authority in the church is to claim the gospel of Jesus Christ. Luther declared that the gospel was the only true treasure of the church. Or, as Peter said to the man begging for money at the gate of the temple: "I have no silver or gold, but what I have I give you; in the name of Jesus Christ of Nazareth, stand up and walk" (Acts 3:6). When the church hears and receives the new life in Christ, celebrates the new life in worship and fellowship, and engages in witness and service, it is in a position to claim the authority given to it by Christ. Such a point of view allows us to also see that if the church does not claim this authority, it cannot be the church. Without this authority there would be no witness, no participation in the new creation, no celebration or service. Authority is derived from the gospel and only by claiming it can the church accept its apostolic mission to baptize, preach, teach, and trust in the presence and promise of Christ.

A Case Study: Ordination

The issue of authority is illustrated by the debate over the basis of ordained ministry. To set the stage for the discussion, we need to recall the state of ordained ministry at the time of Luther and Calvin. The medieval church had officially approved the expansion of the sacraments to seven, with one being ordination to holy orders. This reflected the theology that the church was a spiritual institution derived from the incarnation of Christ. In effect, the church was a two-story structure: the lower level consisted of the laity; the higher level consisted of religious orders, organized in ranks from monks and priests to bishops and the bishop of Rome, the Pope. Christians therefore had the opportunity to choose the *religious life,* or life as *laity.* The ordained represented a higher level of being in the structure of the church. Such ordination possessed legitimate authority only if consecrated by bishops in direct succession with the apostles.

The Reformers rejected this view of the church and ordination. Luther held that baptism conferred on all Christians a priesthood of all believers, whereby they are called to serve God and neighbor. This meant a radical shift in the way one thinks of the church. Instead of a vast vertical hierarchy with gradations of being and authority, now all Christians are on the same horizontal line, whatever their vocation, equal in status and calling. Moreover, church and state were understood as two kingdoms ordained by God, one authorized to proclaim the gospel and the other to exercise the sword for civil order. The justification for the great inequalities of the medieval church, as well as its claims to worldly powers, was gone. What then happened to ordination? This office was retained as a practice or rite for the well being of the church, that is, for the exercise of tasks necessary for the church's life. The three tasks that received attention were preaching, teaching, and administration of the sacraments. General governance of the church was shared between the bishops, pastors, and lay leaders, sometimes ordained as elders and deacons. The Protestant view of ordination came to be seen as functional in contrast to the medieval emphasis on a higher level of being. (One should note that there is nothing in this theory of ordained leadership which would prevent churches from determining that other tasks are necessary for the church's life, establishing the requirements for such, and proceeding to ordain persons called by the church. For example, one can make the case that leadership in health care institutions, social service agencies, agencies of public witness or teaching in church-related institutions constitutes part of the essential mission of the church. In the past, the test for ordination has usually been preaching and administration of the sacraments in congregations. If this is taken in a strict sense, ordination would be denied to these other forms of service.)

If we fast forward to mid-twentieth century, Protestants supported what might be called the functional view of ordination for many reasons. It was, after all, their traditional view and clearly separated Protestants from Roman Catholics. Ordination conferred no special status but was a calling to serve in the ministry of preaching, teaching, and sacraments. But it also allowed for other tasks or functions to be added, out of interest or demanded by church bodies. Thus pastors were also expected to be proficient in church leadership, finance, evangelism, counseling, programs for children and youth, issues of social justice, as well as ministry to the aged. All of these were understood as functions, i.e., things to do, which in turn require technical proficiency. The functional view also allowed a new generation of pastors to react against two older models of ministry: the authority figure; and the holy person set apart from the congregation. But these reactions encountered a problem. Try as they may, even Protestants found it hard to refrain from placing their pastors on a higher level and expecting them to model the Christian faith. When this carried over to the pastor's spouse and children, considerable stress was created in the pastor's family. Nevertheless, pastors and laity were not sure they wanted either of these older models for ministry, especially if the older models excluded the laity from decision making or isolated the pastor. In seminaries, the last thing most students wanted was to be different or to have their families set apart or above everyone else, subject to special scrutiny. In fact, the 1960s brought great pressure for pastors to be involved in the world, be it the arts, politics, or the causes for social justice. Thus from several sources, there was justification for the functional view.[16]

16. One of the problems created by the functional view is that it equates the value of ordained persons with what they do. On these terms, regional and national officers are equated with the dispensing of goods and services. While this sounds good, what happens if a time arises when pastors and congregations say that they do not want those goods and services? When this happens, the existence of these officers is called into ques-

But the functional view encountered serious problems. First, church members did indeed expect their pastor to be a model of the Christian life. They thought it reasonable to have a pastor who believed the message, was spiritually centered, honest and faithful in personal relations, and embodied what might be called moral character. Whether they simply wanted their pastor to be a representative Christian or to exceed the standards of the laity was not clear. What was clear was that defining ministry only in terms of *doing* certain tasks seemed incomplete; members expected the pastor to *embody* the new life. Second, the more one reflects upon the Christian life, one is drawn to the Pauline idea that doing proceeds out of being. That is to say, what we do in our relations with others, especially in preaching and teaching, draws upon the values and commitments that form the person. Love, kindness, and forgiveness grow out of the person who has known these forms of grace. The ability to connect the gospel with the lives of persons in a sermon grows out of a person who is already connected to the gospel. From this perspective, it is quite appropriate to expect a pastor *to be Christian* before he or she can *do the work* of Christian ministry. This is not to overlook the fact that every pastor discovers new insights into faith by the practice of ministry and learns from others. But the point is still valid: somewhere along the way the functional view lost sight of the fact that those ordained are expected to embody the gifts and graces of the Christian life—not necessarily as the only ones to do so, or as the best representative, but simply in their own way as they journey with other pilgrims. Third, if all of this seems too abstract, consider the impact of violations of trust by pastors. Roman Catholics have had to struggle with the abuse of children by priests, Protestants have had to struggle with the infidelity of married pastors. The damage—personal and economic— to families is great and in many cases underestimated. The damage to congregations is also great. Besides the anger and disappointment, there is a break in trust that takes years to repair. These difficult experiences raised the issue of personal integrity as a prerequisite for ministry, alongside of technical competence.

---

tion. The alternative would be to see these officers, as well as pastors, called to represent in their person the unity of Christ, or to witness to the presence of God in the world. This, however, moves away from the purely functional view, where the offices are reduced to the quality and quantity of goods and services.

What then would it mean to rethink the office of ordained ministry? Once again we must return to the origin of the church. The church
originates in the gift and promise of God's saving power in this world.
In Christ we are reconciled to one another and to God, and know the
first freedom from the powers of sin and death. All Christians, therefore,
are called to represent in their lives and actions the new being of Jesus
Christ. This is especially the case for those who would lead the church in
witness and guidance. The list of tasks or functions must be preceded by
evidence that the person has been formed by the new creation of Christ.[17]
Such persons will have authority not simply because of their knowledge,
leadership talents or technical ability but because they have been formed
by the new life in Christ.

The good news is that for years there have been shifts in this direction by those entering seminary. One reason for this is the increase in the
number of second career students. These students have brought to seminary a wealth of experience and have, in general, proven to be committed
and well qualified. If they differ from their counterparts fifty years ago it
might be this: whereas students in an earlier time came directly out of the
church to pursue ministry in the church, many of the current students are
not as connected to the church but are deeply involved in a spiritual quest
and a process of vocational discernment. For some of these students, the
movement toward seminary came out of a personal crisis where life was
changed by dramatic events. For them the church was a source of gracious support. As a result, they envision their future as participating in
ministries of care for others in need.

In one sense, these students are in tune with the critique of functional education: they want to explore ideas and values for the sake of
self-discovery and personal growth as a prerequisite for ministry. They
are also outspoken in their rejection of a culture consumed by monetary
gain, technological efficiency, and disregard of the suffering of so many.
Thus they are quite open to the concern for personal formation. But in an
ironic way, they present a new challenge for churches wanting to ordain
more ministers. Granted, they do not see seminary simply as a means to
be certified for ordination. The challenge, however, is whether they are
willing and able to embrace the requirements for ministry established
by the church boards and committees. For mainline denominations, this

17. Cf. Carroll, *As One With Authority*, 34–60.

concern is not a parochial or narrow point of view, but rather a concern for candidates to share the faith and ethos of the community. The concern often takes these forms: If students come to seminary on a religious quest or in search of self-enrichment, they will certainly find great resources to support them. But most churches are looking for personal formation that relates to the traditions and congregations of their denomination. For the ordination committees examining many students, the question becomes: Do you know who we are and how does your faith relate to the traditions that form our church? Or, if students come to seminary because the church was a caring place in a time of mid-life crisis, they very often want to define ministry in terms of caring for others. This indeed is an essential part of ministry, but it is not all of ministry. Churches need preachers, teachers, evangelists, and public witnesses as well as care-givers.

In this situation seminaries and churches have work to do. There is little chance of returning to the past where youth groups, church camps and church-related colleges formed students in the faith and ethos of particular churches before students got to seminary. For forty years colleges and universities have rushed to offer preparation for careers, with less and less emphasis on broad education in the arts, literature, religion, philosophy, ethics, and history (i.e., studies involving self-discovery and consideration of values). Since those graduating have not used four years to engage in self-discovery or to explore issues of faith and moral values, it is not surprising that we find many people dissatisfied with their first career, struggling with a personal crisis. Here lies a significant area of ministry for churches: to provide a safe place where young and middle-age adults may voice their frustrations with work and culture in search of new commitments. This part of the population will contain some people who will find themselves called to ministry. Congregations need to look with the eyes of faith and place before them such a call. For the seminaries, this means that much greater emphasis needs to be placed on programs of personal formation, spiritual growth and immersion in the church tradition of candidates for ordination. Those seminaries that emphasize students being in care of one's church, the practice of worship and spiritual development, and the ability to relate with others—as well as excellence in required studies—will be best prepared to deal with the new student population. We need to bear in mind that the students reflect the great crisis in churches and culture. It should not surprise us that some students appear unchurched or are refugees from oppressive traditions. As long as the culture confronts individuals with conflicting values and disregards their real needs, we will have people cautiously making inquiries of seminaries. They may not be as bold as St. Bernard, who presented himself with friends and relatives at the gate of the Cistercian monastery, or as desperate as Luther, seeking refuge among the Augustinians, but they are in search of a new life.

This discussion exposes the fact that there is more than one issue involved in the authority of ordained ministry. There is the need to balance the traditional functional view with that of embodying new life. There is also the need to balance the current quest for personal growth and self-actualization with the need of churches to ordain persons formed in their faith and ethos. In many respects the interest of the churches for formation in their own tradition is antithetical to the general cultural value of personal autonomy. After all, in America it is generally recognized that the individual has a right to believe as she/he sees fit. The church, however, speaks the language of one who called us to seek first the Kingdom of God. Thus it is crucial for churches to have the courage to affirm the authority of their faith and practice. There are, however, enough cases where individuals refuse to conform to church traditions because of exclusive policies regarding race, gender, sexual orientation, abortion, or peacemaking. These cases mean that one cannot make a unilateral judgment in favor of church traditions over individual conscience. But it is still worth making the point that the authority for ministry can not lie solely in the rights of the individual. Ordained ministry has authority derived from the church's centers of authority: church practice, Scripture, creeds, church governance, and landmark decisions. Even when these are used to justify repressive policies, in fact especially in such cases, we need to appeal to them in search of a more authentic form of witness.

four

Christ Is the Morning Star:
An Eschatological Vision for Our Time

Christ is the Morning Star,
Who when the night of this world is past,
Brings to his saints the promise of the light of life
And opens everlasting day.

—Venerable Bede, 8th c.

A Loss of Vision

Our culture is nearsighted. In economics we look for the quick return. Personal savings have been down as we search for the good life now. Education becomes the acquisition of technical data for immediate results rather than formation of character and long term growth. Religion becomes the American Cultural Religion that is all about my interests. Such practice means the loss of a larger perspective, driven by God's purposes and the goal of history.

To make the point, consider the concern regarding the question: Does God love me? The assumption here is that God exists, but for little purpose than to meet our needs and love us. So what are the answers we hear? On the conservative side, the answer is quite emphatic: Yes, *if* you comply with our expectations regarding participation in church and our standards for personal life. In effect, a place in heaven is reserved for you, if you meet the tests at the doors of churches. The problem here is not that something might be expected of us, but the way the divine love is doled out as a reward for compliance with set beliefs and practices. As history shows, this restriction of God's love only to those qualified leads to domination of the faithful by rules and authoritarian leaders. It inevitably produces many who are wounded and forced out of churches as refugees. To avoid all this, and out of protest against such ecclesial presumption, the liberal response to the question is an unqualified Yes. Of course God loves you; God's love is unconditional so live life to the fullest. Here the problem is not the praise of God's unmerited grace, but the silence regarding how love draws us into circles of love and service. The main point, however, is that both of these answers reduce Christian faith to the question whether God loves us. Neither spends much time expecting us to expand our near-sightedness in order to glimpse the larger purposes of God. Jesus' words about losing one's life for the Kingdom of God are not a favorite text for American religion.[1]

Defining the Problem: Multiple Sources; Multiple Interpretations.

It is easy to argue that a vision of the goal of history is necessary for the faith and life of the church, but quite difficult to reach agreement on what it shall be. In the past two centuries, Christians in America have been basically divided over whether or not to affirm some form of Armageddon, involving the final confrontation of Christ and the forces of evil. Such a vision presupposes the radical opposition between God and Satan, as well as the possibility of determining the date for such a final event. One can find advocates for such a view among conservative churches, but especially among religious groups formed around this issue, such as Shakers, Millerites, Seventh-day Adventists, Jehovah's Witnesses, Bible and

---

1. Some will object that God's purposes are in fact a major theme in popular religion, pointing to the bestselling books by Rev. Rick Warren. The question that needs to be asked is whether the word purpose is being used as a motivational technique to inspire people to some purpose that will give meaning to their life, or are they speaking in theological terms about the purposes of God.

Independent Churches, and TV preachers of prophecy. This view even extends into American foreign policy, since the State of Israel becomes a piece in the puzzle to determine the final event. On the other side would be those wanting to affirm a future defined by God's rule and hope in the coming of the Kingdom of God. It would include a general hope in the Second Coming of Christ, but without setting a date for the end of the world or describing a final, violent confrontation. The question, therefore, is which version shall we affirm?

Let us begin by defining key terms. The Greek word *eschaton* refers to the final time or goal, whereas *apocalypse* refers to what is revealed. But there is no precise agreement as to how the words shall be used. Sometimes all references to the future, the intervention of the Spirit, or conflict with Satan are considered examples of apocalyptic thought. At other times, apocalyptic refers to a specific core of ideas: messages to the faithful hidden in symbolic language, a clear division between good and evil, predictions of the a final battle (Armageddon) at a specific date, leading to a new age or millennium of peace. I propose that it is more useful to define apocalyptic in this restricted sense. If the category is not restricted, then all ideas regarding the goal of history are lumped under the general heading of apocalyptic. The problem, however, is that not all ideas regarding the goal of history involve the clear cut division of good and evil, dating the end time, or a violent conflict.[2] As a consequence, I shall use eschatology (i.e., language and theories about the final goal) as the broadest category for speaking of the future. By contrast, apocalyptic will be used as a specific form of eschatological thought. On these terms, not all forms of eschatology are apocalyptic, but apocalyptic ideas are a specific form of eschatology.

How does this distinction help us understand key passages in the New Testament? In general it means that references in the Gospels and Paul, which refer to God, Satan and the coming Kingdom fit into a broad eschatological framework, whereas the Book of Revelation is a striking example of an apocalyptic vision. Let us look at some of the eschatological passages first.

---

2. In general, this approach is supported by the way John Dominic Crossan deals with the two categories in *Jesus, A Revolutionary Biography*, 40ff. Cf. Borg, *Meeting Jesus for the First Time*, 29ff. and 103.

A wide range of passages refer to the Kingdom of God and the tension between Christ and Satan without implying an apocalyptic point of view.[3] Here one could mention Jesus' announcement of the Kingdom of God in Mark 1:14. Jesus makes clear that the appropriate response to this event is repentance and belief, not preparing for the final judgment and the end of the world. Also included here would be the account of the temptations in Matthew and Luke, as well as the exorcism of demons, along with the debate over the meaning of such an event (cf. Luke 11:14–23).[4] Most important, Mark 13, sometimes called "The Little Apocalypse," is now considered to represent a traditional eschatological framework, rather than the classic apocalyptic view. E. P. Sanders argues that the hope of divine intervention was common among Jews of the first century, but this did not mean the end of the world.[5] While Mark 13 does indeed speak of terrible signs, it does not necessarily imply the end of all things. Finally, it is significant that Jesus does not engage in speculation about the end time, nor are his teachings about the Kingdom of God formulated in apocalyptic terms. When he is opposed by his fellow Jews and the Romans, he does not speak the language of absolute polarization. He weeps for Jerusalem, given its poor response, but he does not call down upon it ultimate punishment. In the great commission from the resurrected Christ, the disciples are to teach, baptize, and make disciples, with a promise of his presence until the end; they are not to forsake the world in preparation for Armageddon.

A similar appraisal can be made of Paul's comments about the tension between Christ and Satan, light and darkness and the coming of Christ. These passages lack the distinctive marks of apocalyptic discourse: prediction of the end, absolute polarization of good and evil, and a violent confrontation. In fact, Paul begins a process of adjustments regarding the expectation of Christ's return: in this time of waiting, people will have to work and it may even be better for them to marry rather then put off such concerns.[6]

3. Cf. Sanders, *The Historical Figure of Jesus*, 169–88 and Borg, *Meeting Jesus*, 96–103.

4. Cf. the treatment of the temptations by E. P. Sanders, where these narratives are not judged to be apocalyptic: Sanders, *Historical Figure*, 112–17.

5. Ibid., 174ff.

6. One can find support for a non-apocalyptic view of Christian faith in an unexpected place, namely, the doctrine of sin. By and large, the Christian view of sin, so strongly influenced by Paul and Augustine, stands as a defense against the dualism of

Things are quite different when we turn to the Book of Revelation. Here we have a thoroughgoing apocalyptic vision: polarization of good and evil, prediction of the end time (Armageddon), leading to a new age. It leaves little doubt that the world has fallen under the power of evil forces. In such a time of persecution, Christians receive a message hidden in symbols of the coming warfare that will rescue the faithful and usher in a new age. Since this Book is included in the New Testament, it creates a serious problem for those who affirm the primacy of Scripture. Sooner or later we are going to have to make a decision about the role this Book should play in the faith and life of the church. Before we make that decision, it will be helpful to review how this issue relates to long standing divisions between Christians.

The Debate over Apocalyptic Thought

The Book of Revelation has been a major factor in the division of American traditions. Like the Culture War, it creates a network of alliances among the opposing camps. This means that issues merge in unpredictable ways so that it is sometimes difficult to identify cause and effect.[7] Several examples make the point:

- American churches line up on two sides over this issue: In support of apocalyptic ideas and language are those named above as well as conservative Baptist, Holiness, and Pentecostal traditions. Opposition comes from mainline Protestant groups and Roman Catholics.

---

apocalypticism. The problem with the human condition is not caused by an eternal evil force, nor because human beings or anything in the world is inherently evil. Following the refusal of Genesis 3 to blame the serpent, Augustine sees the source of our problem in our misuse of the things of this world, or rebellion against God. The point is that in spite of all the criticism of the doctrine of sin as being negative and pessimistic, in fact its underlying premise is optimistic: since sin is not inherent to human nature, humankind can be redeemed.

7. The image of Culture Wars became popular through the writing of James Davison Hunter, who argued that conservatives and liberals are divided by multiple religious, social and political issues extended over time. As a consequence a discussion regarding one issue inevitably spills over into other issues and is complicated by old wounds and antagonisms. Hunter gave primary attention to the way the divide originates in different views of authority, though I think it is also caused by opposing views of freedom, sin, and salvation. Cf. Hunter, *Culture Wars*.

- Apocalyptic ideas have more appeal to certain audiences. Since these ideas arise out of times of persecution, they are attractive to anyone experiencing hardship and crisis. They resonate with those who consider themselves outsiders, disinherited or alienated from majority culture and especially organized religion. Visions of the faithful being rescued from persecution by the powerful, or of an end time that reverses all relations of status and power, appeal to many people. But one must guard against thinking that only the poor or powerless are attracted to apocalyptic ideas. In a large and complex society, one does not need to languish in prison or be economically impoverished for these ideas to catch the imagination. Everyone can claim moments of exclusion or victimization. For example, in the 1960s, some of the anti-war protestors who embraced apocalyptic rhetoric were children of privilege. Twenty to fifty years later, many of the anti-tax leaders who come from positions of wealth and influence nevertheless speak of the government as evil, suggesting a polarization beyond repair. The point is that people feeling estranged from other parts of the society or living with anger may easily identify with apocalyptic thinking. We also need to note that people do not automatically give up confidence in apocalyptic rhetoric because their social or economic context improves. It would appear that the allure of apocalyptic ideas persists through many generations, long after the crisis which originated the first interest, due to the power of traditional practices and loyalties.

- The rivalry in this debate mirrors the competing approaches to the study of the Bible. One side insists on the inerrancy of the text while the other side prefers to think of the texts giving witness to the Word of God revealed in Israel and Jesus Christ. The latter position relies on historical and linguistic study of the Bible, allowing it to see the limitations of apocalyptic rhetoric and images. The former position discounts much of this, in its attempt to apply the Book of Revelation to the present situation.[8]

- While conservatives have been more prone to transfer the Book of Revelation to the present situation, both sides show a willingness to

8. Cf. the analysis of the on going tensions between critical Biblical scholars and Biblical prophesy in Greg Carey, *Elusive Apocalypse*.

use the imagery as they see appropriate. This is because so many of the images are open ended: The beast could be the Roman Empire, Nazi Germany or the Soviet Communist Empire, or for that matter, whatever one opposes, such as the military-industrial complex, Western economic imperialism, or the National Council of Churches (i.e., organized religion).[9]

- Finally, the two sides represent quite different understandings of the relation of church and culture. But their positions are complex, revealing within each a high level of ambiguity. Take the conservative position: In general these churches are from the independent or free church tradition, which historically never were state churches and opposed such an alliance. As a result they carry an historic memory of being outsiders, set apart from the established churches. Such a position would fit in quite well with the antagonism between the suffering Christians in the Book of Revelation and the government, represented by Rome. In the current Culture War, these groups openly denounce liberal and government establishments, but quite unexpectedly they also seek to turn the tables and gain control of government. Thus, instead of wanting nothing to do with the beast and praying for its destruction, many are devoting time and money to acquire the power of the beast, i.e., establish in Washington the rule of white, English speaking, true believers. The liberal side is just as ambivalent, though in different ways. Since mainline churches descended from state churches in Europe and brought with them to America a theocratic vision, they have more positive attitudes toward government. But they have become fierce advocates of separation of church and state. They are also quick to see the oppressive nature of American society and the way the state joins hand in hand with religious, social and economic forces. Thus on this side of the Culture War, there is also ambiguity: a general respect and support for the state ordained by God, coupled with the need to keep church and state separate and to criticize repressive policies.

9. Cf. Ibid., 32–24, and 163–75 on the on the use of Revelation by both liberationists and Bible prophecy.

This survey of issues reminds us that one cannot ask about the goal of history without: making a decision about apocalyptic ideas; becoming entangled with longstanding divisions in American religion.

Claiming Christ's Future

The Limits of the Apocalyptic Vision

There is no denying the attraction of the apocalyptic vision. It not only names the terrible things which are happening but gives us a reason why. And it declares that God is going to do something about it. Indeed, the divine intervention shall be nothing less than the destruction of the old order and the creation of a new time of righteousness. But this vision has serious limits.

The first is that apocalyptic visions are always tied to a specific time of crisis that passes. The Book of Revelation was written in the context of the persecution of Christians by the Roman Empire—which no longer exists. Moreover, the predictions of the end of the world in a cosmic struggle and glorious triumph have not happened. It is a message confined to a specific time in the first century, with predictions that failed. Why then should churches today use the apocalyptic framework to think about the future? One response is that of the Millerites. When William Miller's prediction of the end of the world in 1834 proved wrong, some of his followers said he miscalculated. But the second try also proved incorrect. This prompted some, who came to be known as Seventh-day Adventists, to argue that it would not occur until the true Sabbath was observed.[10] Another response is to start all over again with new applications of apocalyptic images. This has been the case in the last 60 years, where the calculations have been reloaded with data regarding the Soviet Union, the State of Israel and/or natural catastrophes. But at some point, is it not appropriate to say that these visions and applications simply don't work? God has not ended everything; the earth continues on its course through its seasons. One needs to ask whether the promise to Noah is more relevant than the vision of Revelation. There are other ways besides apocalyptic visions to call the church to resist the powers of evil.

10. Hudson, *Religion in America*, 194–97.

A second limitation arises from the origin of apocalyptic ideas. In general, these ideas gain usage in Jewish thought during and after the Babylonian exile (sixth century B.C.). E. P. Sanders reminds us of the similarities between such ideas and dualism of Zoroastrian and Manichaean beliefs.[11] In such a world view, there is an ultimate division between good and evil stemming from two divine forces. This dualism allows for the conclusion that the created order is flawed because it was formed by evil forces. This also implies that it is irredeemable. When these ideas emerge in apocalyptic thought, they inevitably lead to conflict only resolved by ultimate warfare. One can only wonder how these ideas could be compatible with Jewish faith. If, with Genesis and the prophets, there is only one God who has created all things and called them good, how could such apocalyptic ideas be tolerated? The answer lies in two sources.

The first is the great tension created by believing in only one God and affirming the reality of sin and evil. The tension is almost intolerable and is never completely resolved, as Genesis illustrates. In Genesis 3 it is clear that one cannot blame evil on a second god, since there is only one God. Nor can one blame it on something wrong with the creation itself, since it is good. This leaves only one alternative, namely, that moral evil arises through disobedience (i.e., the bad choices humans make). But this solution is complicated by the fact that God allowed them to make the choice and they were tempted by the serpent. While not intended, the story leaves the door ajar for believers to place the cause of evil on other spiritual forces, even though they are less than the one true God. Blaming demons not only gets human beings off the hook, in some ways it deflects the blame from God. This helps us understand how ideas of Satan and demonic powers could be acceptable in Jewish apocalyptic thought. By the time of Jesus, there is a general recognition of demonic forces which defy God even though they are subordinate to God.[12]

The second reason why apocalyptic ideas find acceptance is the occasion of extreme crisis. When human suffering and the evils that cause it reach such unimaginable proportions, it is possible for the faithful to wonder whether something really has gone wrong with the created order itself. The world seems no longer to be interrupted by individual acts of selfishness or violence, but by larger than life forces—dare we even say de-

11. Sanders, *Historical Figure*, 114–17.

12. Ibid., 114–15.

monic forces on a cosmic scale. In such cases the opposition between good and evil has become absolute and there is no chance for reconciliation. It is in that moment that the images of the books of Daniel or Revelation suddenly come alive. If all this seems unimaginable, ask yourself why *The Lord of the Rings* or *The Chronicles of Narnia* were written in the period of world wars in the last century by Oxford professors? There are times when a more likely explanation of moral disorder and world catastrophe is found in the imagery of a contest between good and evil, which can be resolved only through a final conflict.[13]

But explaining why apocalyptic ideas arise should not deter us from seeing that they are ultimately destructive of Jewish and Christian faith. Once one begins to speak of two divine sources of creative energy—one good and one evil—and draws the further conclusion that the only solution is the destruction of the enemy, one moves outside of the mainstream of Jewish and Christian faith. The early Christian church saw this danger at numerous points and in each case rejected it. In one case, Marcion proposed a dualism of two gods and wanted the church to reject the entire Old Testament. In the case of Gnosticism, the church faced a religious option that posited multiple gods, good and evil, with finite existence deemed to be evil. For the Gnostics, the only solution was to escape the sufferings and evils of physical life by being resurrected to the realm of a pure spiritual existence. Against Marcion and the Gnostics, the early Christians affirmed one God, a good creation, the reality of sin, but also

---

13. One finds apocalyptic imagery readily available in American popular culture. In the original Star Wars trilogy, the underlying assumption is the absolute polarization of good and evil. The only thing one can do with the evil forces is kill them. But then at the end, it turns out that Darth Vader is the young hero's father, who turned from good to evil. In an instant, the whole framework changes to the biblical images of fall and redemption. If good can be corrupted, then it also can be redeemed. Another example appears in the difference between the book *Cold Mountain* and its movie version. In the book, the hero is killed by accident by a young man who ends up marrying the servant to the heroine. The book ends with the survivors gathered together for a meal—a most suggestive image. The message is clear: life is tragic; even though we do terrible things unintentionally, we are reconciled by the power of love and forgiveness. The movie, however, was unwilling to affirm such an ending. Therefore, in its version, the hero and the villain kill one another, reminiscent of the perpetual warfare between good and evil. When the movie closes with the common meal, there is no resolution. They are only victims choosing to press on. One can only wonder whether Hollywood thought Americans could not handle the tragic ending of the book, but would require the easy answer of the perpetual warfare of good and evil.

the reality of redemption in this physical world.[14] Given this history of the early church, one finds good reason to be cautious about, if not totally opposed to, apocalyptic ideas and predictions.

Of course the response may be offered: if apocalyptic ideas are so opposed to the Christian view of creation, sin, and redemption, why then are they present in the New Testament? I am prepared to consider the possibility that we will never know why the early church included the Book of Revelation in the New Testament.[15] The most likely explanation is that, given the destruction of the Jerusalem temple in AD 70 and the ongoing persecution of Christians by the Roman empire, many felt that these images reflected the world in which they lived and the conviction that an imminent divine judgment was the only option.[16] But this explanation only takes us back to the question: Why should such a vision be applicable today?

I find it instructive that not all parts of the New Testament are of one mind on the embrace of apocalyptic ideas. Consider the way Jesus is presented in the synoptic Gospels. Whether the following examples reflect words directly from Jesus, the Gospel writers, or the early church is a continuing debate. But in any case, this is the way Jesus is remembered. As argued in the previous section, Jesus' teachings regarding the Kingdom of God avoid the excesses of apocalyptic thought. It is also instructive to consider the Book of Acts. If it is an accurate glimpse of the post-resurrection community, it is lacking in apocalyptic images and predictions. To be sure, the quotation from Joel includes the reference to blood, fire and smoke, and upon being condemned Stephen has a vision of the Son of Man at the right hand of God. But these are left undeveloped. All of Peter's sermons follow the pattern of what E. P. Sanders calls the history

14. Compare again how the Christian doctrine of sin functions as a defense against the ideas of Marcion and the Gnostics, which presuppose a dualism of good and evil. By insisting that the origin of moral evil lies somewhere between temptation and human willfulness, it stands as a powerful reminder that the problem is not in cosmic forces, the enemies we have demonized, but in us.

15. One large area of discussion is whether key passages in the Gospels, especially those related to the Son of Man, are directly from the lips of Jesus or insertions by the early church. If one agrees with a writer like John Dominic Crossan that these sayings are not from Jesus, then to some extent they lose their authority. But one still must explain why they are in the gospels, which is usually done by reference to the times (cf. Crossan, *Jesus*, 40–53).

16. Carey, *Elusive Apocalypse*, 136–64.

of redemption: As God revealed saving power in Abraham, Moses, David, and the prophets, so now redemption comes in Jesus.[17]

Let us pause to review: Thus far I have tried to make the case that the church needs a vision of the future lest it turn in upon itself. This was followed by a brief overview of the challenges involved in constructing an eschatological vision: the problem of apocalyptic thought and the resulting divisions within American churches. These matters form the context for proposing an alternative vision of the future. As with all major issues relating to the church, solutions are always proposed in the context of need and controversy.

The Future Christ Brings

Whether we ever resolve the problems connected to eschatology in the New Testament, the fact is that churches make decisions about the future. It is in the context of affirmations about the future, or the embarrassment caused by silence about the future, that the following proposal is offered as the fourth essential component of the church:

The church is a community which claims a future defined by God's act in Jesus Christ. Therefore the church is a community of hope.

To see the future in terms of Jesus Christ requires that we know who he is and what has happened in his life, crucifixion, and resurrection. In the first chapter I have summarized the meaning of Jesus in terms of the affirmation of new life, based on the primacy of grace and the intervention of holiness. This I believe is consistent with the Gospels as well as Paul. But Jesus can also be described in terms of the language he uses. In the synoptic Gospels Jesus uses the image of the Kingdom of God to describe what God is doing. For first-century Jews, this image connects with the rule of God over Israel, where the first King was always God. It also connects with a shared faith that God's Kingdom is also in heaven. What Jesus declares is that God's rule, tied to Israel and in heaven, has now come near to all who would repent and believe. For the early Christians, the signs of this Kingdom breaking into our lives on earth are the well known ones from the life of Jesus, especially the decisive ones of Holy Week:

17. Sanders, *Historical Figure*, 80–88.

- Jesus astounds observers by healing and casting out demons.
- He gathers men, women and children, rich and poor, to share table fellowship.
- By his actions and teachings he protests against a world of power and oppression, calling his followers to take up an alternative set of values, which even they do not understand.
- In his resistance to temptation and fidelity to God in his suffering and death, Jesus stands as the faithful witness to the Rule of God.
- In his resurrection God vindicates the crucified and raises him to be Lord.
- With the bestowal of the Spirit, the believers are empowered to be the community of Christ on earth, proclaiming by Word and deed the good news.

Once we are clear about what has happened in Jesus, we discover that the goal of history arises out of these events. It is not something which we create, but is the inevitable gift contained in the story of Jesus itself. It has power to attract our hearts and minds and draw us into the future of the world because it is already present in Jesus. But here we must recognize that the power of the goal is also derived from God's faithfulness in the past. In this way the eschatological goal of the future gathers into its field of vision the affirmation that Jesus is the fulfillment of the promises of God to Israel. The new life in the Kingdom on earth is now placed in the historical context of the covenants of Israel. This becomes apparent in the sermons of Peter, Stephen and Paul. But it is dramatically illustrated in the three great prayers of praise and thanksgiving in Luke 1 and 2. From the mouths of Mary, Zechariah, and Simeon the meaning of the births of John and Jesus is made clear:

- praise is given for God's faithfulness to these persons, but also to Israel. (Luke 1:47–48, 54–55, 68–78 and 2:29–32.)
- God's judgment falls upon those who rule with power and pride.
- The salvation now to be revealed shall elevate the poor and lowly, feed the hungry (Luke 1:68), bestow the forgiveness of sins, let light shine in darkness and resist death (Luke 1:77).

- Those drawn into this Kingdom shall serve with holiness and righteousness (Luke 1:73).

As the synoptic writers proceed to tell the story of Jesus, what Jesus says and does is placed in the context of God's promises to Israel. Two examples make the point: In Luke 4:16–21 Jesus reads from Isaiah in the synagogue in Nazareth:

> The Spirit of the Lord is upon me, because he has anointed me to bring good news to the poor. He has sent me to proclaim release to the captives and recovery of sight to the blind, to let the oppressed go free, and proclaim the year of the Lord's favor.

In Luke 7:18–23 the followers of John the Baptist ask if Jesus is the one promised. Jesus responds: "Go and tell John what you see . . ." referring again to the signs of salvation announced in Isaiah (and for Luke, the three prayers of Luke 1–2).

If the new life in Jesus is part of God's purpose, fulfilling the promises to Israel, then it necessarily points to the future. God is always the One who was, is, and shall be. The salvation embodied in Jesus Christ is not an accident, nor an isolated event. It gathers together past and future into the new life of the community of Christ. The creative power of the coming of Christ does not die on the cross, nor can it be contained in the present, or even in the community which bears His name. It moves ahead of us (as Christ was always moving ahead of the disciples) toward the future goal. Just as Jesus Christ points to the future, so the future draws us forward into a new way of faith and action in this world.

This presents us with a quite unexpected but deliberate play on words: to see the future we must look to the present as a sign of the future. Such a proposal means that the future is the unfolding of what is fulfilled and has begun in Jesus Christ. Consider the way the early church frames the whole issue of the future. To begin with, instead of looking for the coming of the Son of Man—the heavenly being mentioned in the Book of Daniel—the church looks to the crucified and risen Jesus who will come again. Christians are called to see, celebrate, and pray for the coming of the Kingdom—the very Kingdom Jesus announced and embodied. The new age, therefore, is not a time of preparation for Armageddon, but a time of missionary endeavor to preach, teach, and baptize (Matt 28). In this time, the faithful are called to prepare and wait for the time when God will gather together all things in Christ (Eph. 1:10; cf. Col. 1:20). In such a time they have the promise of Christ's presence and are empowered by the Spirit of Christ.

The best way to unravel the logic of what has been proposed is to look at cases. Let us begin with Ephesians 1–2. The first thing that catches our eye is the insistence that what has happened in Jesus (that is, our salvation) was intended by God before creation. In Ephesians 1:3–15, five verses boldly speak of God's intention. Note what God does:

- "... chose us in Christ before the foundation of the world." (1:4)

- "...destined us for adoption ..." (1:5)

- "... made known to us the mystery of his will ..." (1:9)

- "... as a plan for the fullness of time, to gather up all things in him ..." (1:10)

- "In Christ we have also obtained an inheritance, having been destined according to the purpose of him who accomplishes all things ..." (1:11)

While this passage does not mention Abraham, Moses, or David, it is assumed that the Father of Jesus Christ is the God of Israel: the salvation revealed in Jesus is the fulfillment of God's promises.

The second thing about this passage is that the saving power revealed in Jesus is so overwhelming that it constitutes a new point of departure for the way the believers think about the future. What is now given in Christ may be extended to describe the goal of history. In this case, the reality of our adoption as children of God is extended to the future: "With all wisdom and insight he [God] has made known to us the mystery of his will, according to his good pleasure that he set forth in Christ, as a plan for the fullness of time, to gather up all things in him, things in heaven and things on earth" (Eph 1:8–11). The same kind of extension occurs elsewhere. In Romans 8, Paul declares that since the love of God binds us to God in Christ, therefore by extension, the future may be described as continuing in that love: Neither death nor any of the powers of this world "can separate us from the love of God in Christ Jesus our Lord." A final example is John's vision of the goal of history: As Jesus reveals the love and truth of God the Father, so that love and truth flows from Jesus to the disciples and from them to the world, that the world might believe (cf. John 17:21). The future is therefore described as the extension of what has already taken place in the encounter of Jesus and the disciples. This is justifiable because the new reality takes precedence over all other realities: the daily struggle for survival and safety or all those worldly powers which claim to control our future. An eschatological vision is not the denial of such realities, but the affirmation that the future shall ultimately be defined by the God who raised Jesus Christ.

A striking example of allowing God to define the future is found in Isaiah. In Isaiah 11 the goal of history is described as a peaceable kingdom. In one respect, this image seems to be the work of human fancy, since it moves so completely beyond anything we have experienced. It is not a direct extension of the present to the future, from some being reconciled to all being reconciled. But is this not Isaiah's point: the redemption of Israel as a covenant community was not a human expectation. Just as God's new creation of a faithful people in a world of chaos and violence is unbelievable, so God shall continue to transform the world in ways which we cannot imagine. Thus these images reveal both the disorder of the present world and our hope that it be redeemed. What if all the killing stopped? We cannot imagine now a world without swords, but what if they were all transformed into plows and pruning hooks (Is. 2:4)?

It is appropriate to mention here how this eschatological vision lies at the heart of one family of interpretations of the cross. In my classification of theories of atonement, one group steps back from the immediate concerns of forgiveness, liberation, and reconciliation in order to frame the entire story in terms of God's purposes. To be sure, Jesus means the grace of forgiveness and freedom, of reunion with God and neighbor. But underlying all of these benefits of Christ is an issue relating to God. The ultimate rationale for the history of saving power lies in God's purposes. So, both Athanasius and Anselm ask the question: What was God to do? For Athanasius, God becomes human in order to renew humankind according to the divine intention. For Anselm, the incarnation is the necessary consequence of God's faithfulness to the divine purpose. The harmony and beauty of the world shall be restored. From a different perspective, Schleiermacher considered Christ to be the completion of creation, the intervention of new life which shall fulfill the original design. What we find in these three authors, divided by context and so many other issues, is a willingness to think of Christ in terms of God's faithfulness, and then to think of the future in terms of Christ.

To summarize: if then the future is defined in terms of Christ, the church lives in hope. For good reason Paul links faith, hope, and love. To believe in Christ is to claim the future which Christ brings. Christ is the morning star, announcing the new time, precisely at the point when darkness still prevails. He is the one who draws us into a future defined by God's good will. This is not a mission conceived by the church, but mandated by the risen Christ. But for what, you ask, shall we hope? We are to hope precisely for what God has promised: forgiveness of sins in the face of our guilt and despair, reconciliation in the face of our separation, peace in the face of violence, freedom in the face of confinement and domination, and new life as we pray for the coming of the Kingdom. The church therefore is defined by hope: hope as resistance to the kingdoms of this world; hope as the expectation of change; hope as the willingness to be drawn into a life of love and service.

Since hope is part of the essence of the church's faith and life, the church is by definition active in worship, fellowship, education, care, witness, and service. Very often the reason for engaging in these endeavors is to love as we are loved, or out of concern for people in need. These are appropriate motivations but they do not go to the primary motivation, which is the eschatological vision. What has happened to us in Christ, and what we are called to do, grow out of our position in the unfolding of God's purpose. The church is located in the time in which Christ is reconciling us to one another and to God. He is the light which has come into the world in the midst of darkness. The image of the Morningstar is so powerful because it is a double message: the night is ending and the day is beginning. It is an event which happens in spite of our weakness and disbelief. It not only draws us outside of ourselves, but draws us into Christ's future as recipients of grace and agents of reconciliation.

At the outset of the chapter I suggested that when churches step out of the historical framework of an eschatological vision, they lose all sense of a larger purpose. This leads to the American reformulation of Christian faith where it is all about us. Everything turns inward, away from the mindset of participating in Christ's future. When this happens, churches find great comfort in defining the future in terms of our own expectations and values, whether they be expressed in terms of wealth or happiness. In its worst form, the future comes to be defined by our collaboration with the powers of this world, based on more and more consumption and access to more and more goods. But such alternatives are inevitably judged by God's Kingdom. Consider the decisive moment in Mark, where James and John request worldly power when the Kingdom comes on earth. Jesus first affirms the alternative values of fidelity and service by asking if they are able to share his cup. But then to all the disciples Jesus rejects the option of worldly power: "It is not so among you." (Mark 10:43) Both now and at the end, the Kingdom of God represents a reversal of the world's values, not a turning of the tables. The first shall be last and the last shall be first, in spite of the disciples' objections.

One final issue needs to be addressed: Will there be a final judgment separating the good from evil, or shall this age close with all being reconciled to God? This is not an abstract question, given the millions of people who have lost their lives at the hands of evil persons and systems. Of course there are countless sources in the Bible and Christian traditions to enlist on both sides of the question. Here I remain conflicted. On the one hand, I have argued against thinking of the final judgment as a violent end of this world. If I follow consistently what has been proposed, then we must extend what has happened in Jesus Christ: the grace that has been given to us shall be given to all. Moreover, it is not clear to me whether my outrage against ill will and violence is a genuine expression of the need for justice or my own anger and desire for vengeance. On the other hand, I cannot find it in my self to rebuke those who, having suffered such great loss, ask for a divine punishment against evil doers. Nor is it clear that the encounter with the truth and love at the end shall change all hearts. Of course God's power is greater than the ill will of evil doers. But why then did they do their evil acts in the first place? In the Gospels, the rich man turns away in tears from Jesus, grieving his own inability to turn toward the Kingdom of God. In the most sorrowful parable of Jesus, Abraham rejects the plea of the rich man to send someone to his brothers lest they perish. Abraham's final reply is: "If they do not listen to Moses and the prophets, neither will they be convinced even if someone rises from the dead" (Luke 16:31). Matthew 25:31–46 also projects a final judgment. Given such powerful arguments on each side, it would be wise to leave the matter in the hands of God, without attempting to discern the time and terms of God's final judgment. We have a different commission from Christ.[18]

Faith in the Key of Hope

The connection between faith and hope needs further exploration. This is best done by thinking of the way faith creates a new identity for believers and a communal practice for the church. In some ways, the older term piety catches the meaning of faith as personal commitment and communal practice. If we can think of faith in this way, I want to propose that we are living at a time when a new form of faith is emerging—not so much contradicting or replacing older forms, but catching the imagination of believers as they try to come to terms with radical change on a global scale.

Let me begin with a story. When traveling in Italy, I would visit churches in all sorts of places: villages, market towns, cities, and monasteries. Some churches stand in the shadow of cathedrals. Some, more like chapels, are out in the country along roads. As I observed all of these sacred places and the way they were used for daily prayers and worship, culminating with Sabbath services, it made sense to think of the piety at work here as a piety of adoration. The sacred was clearly identified with specific places, because of the people and events attached to them. At these sacred places, the faithful remembered the story of Jesus, which was depicted through the church year. Every church had stations of the cross and usually side chapels for prayers before the crucified Christ, the Virgin Mary, or a martyred saint. In effect, faith had to do with adoring Christ and all those who were faithful and petitioning their aid in our time of need. Such piety culminates in the Roman Mass, where crucifixion and resurrection are remembered in the re-presentation of Christ's sacrifice. It is a richly textured form of piety and appears in all Roman Catholic cultures. It also appears in Eastern Orthodox cultures, but with a different liturgy and music.

---

18. Miroslav Volf offers a powerful argument for Christians to put away violence and engage in reconciliation, while at the same time admitting that the resistance of some to God's will may be so great that they shall be excluded in the final judgment. Cf. *Exclusion and Embrace*, 99–165; 275–306.

A second form of faith emerged in Protestantism, with its emphasis on the proclaimed Word and the response of faith. Here the interplay is between the promise of grace to sinners and the joyous response of faith as trust of the heart. This basic structure is supported by a vernacular Bible, a new catechism, new hymns, and the expansion of the homily into what we now call a sermon. So much confidence was placed on the proclaimed Word in the sermon that it was conceivable for Protestants to have true worship without the sacrament of the Lord's Supper. In this context faith begins with repentance and moves toward the acceptance of grace, calling us to love God and neighbor. The motivation for the Christian life was therefore placed precisely at that point where the believer receives with gratitude the gifts of Christ. For this reason this piety may be called a piety of gratitude. What we believe and do are responses to what God has done for us. Therefore the believer, still prone to forgetfulness and sin, needs to hear again and again the story of saving grace and the call to respond. This piety of gratitude has given form to Lutheran and Reformed traditions, but it also appears among the Anabaptist and Free Church traditions, and the great revivals of the last two centuries.

If the first two forms of piety turn the church's attention to the past in adoring and/or proclaiming the story of Jesus, the third form turns our attention to the present and the future. The basic question is: What is God doing in the world? By framing the question in this way, it not only moves out of the sacred spaces into the world, but turns from the past to the future. Now to be sure, the God who is acting in this world is the God who raised Jesus and bestowed the Spirit on the church. Trying to decide what God is doing today without being clear on what happened in Jesus would be counter-productive. But a new framework for faith is clearly established. The calling of Christians is not completely fulfilled in adoration of Jesus and the saints, nor in proclaiming once again the gospel of grace to needy sinners. It must be about assessing what is happening in our lives and the world around us. Faith therefore, is tested by the call to participate in what God is doing, namely the unfolding of God's glory. Notice the call is not to bring in the Kingdom, or build it, or design it for our time.[19] The

19. H. Richard Niebuhr had little patience for human claims to usher in God's Kingdom. At one point he suggested that the most we can do is clear away the weeds. Even if we wanted to be bolder in describing what we can and should do, the point is that we are responding to what God is already doing. Cf. "The Only Way into the Kingdom of God," *Christian Century*, 447. This comment came in response to his brother's criticism

piety involved here is a piety of glory, revealed in Christ and now in the world about us. It therefore engenders within us hope.

I do not believe that the third form of piety nullifies or eliminates the other two. In fact, I cannot imagine a rich and varied piety for churches that did not have something of all three. But I am struck by how the third attracts the attention of so many people in ways the other two do not seem to do. By its very structure it says clearly that the realm of salvation cannot be confined to the church, but that the church exists to serve God's purpose. By turning our attention to the present and future, it allows us to see the world as the place where Christ is engaging the powers of this world. But here we need to be on guard against a serious misinterpretation. To say that the piety of glory focuses our attention on God's purposes for the world does not mean we are to abandon the church and the ministries of the church gathered out of the world. Nor does it mean that mission is only outside the church. The mission of the church is to be in this world as a community of faith, love, and hope. The hope discussed here cannot be removed from the faithful worship of God, the nurture of children and members, or a host of other things which engender and sustain it.

But as much as we want to hold together the piety of gratitude and the piety of glory, they do in fact move in different directions. The piety of gratitude assumes that the grateful heart, transformed by the grace of God, is the engine that drives the Christian life. For this reason, every call for acts of love or justice is preceded by a reminder of what God has done for us. I say this as one who was raised on such piety and who has preached and taught it all my life. But in an unpredictable way, this piety must count on the motivating engine to run at high speed most of the time, unless it must return to the repair shop to be tuned up and restarted. One unfortunate consequence of this is that worship is then defined primarily as identifying the backsliders with drooping hands and weak knees, rather than celebrating the presence of saving power. By contrast, the piety of glory assumes both what God has done and the fact that we run hot and cold, but focuses our attention on what God is doing in the world. Without overdoing the distinction, this piety asks whether we will join Christ in the unfolding of God's glory, rather than whether we are predisposed toward following him. The motivating power comes from the glory of God, rather than our inner resources. In this light, the question

---

of his article entitled "The Grace of Doing Nothing" *Christian Century*, 378–80.

of vocation or calling suddenly takes on a different meaning, as calling is linked to hope for the world. In one sense, this actually captures Luther's vision of vocation in its many forms: the ministries of the church and the service to our neighbors.[20] It is, as William Stringfellow said years ago, to discern, rely upon, and celebrate the presence of God in the world.[21]

The emergence of this third form of piety is a reminder that the church lives in hope. This hope is not the human virtue of optimism, but the expectation that God will continue to redeem the world. It is based on the conviction that God is faithful and the reality of the unfolding of God's glory. It is sustained by the power of proclamation and glorious music. It should not surprise us that so many Protestants, raised on a rather austere and unimaginative worship life, are overwhelmed by great preaching, or great music, or the richness of high church liturgical traditions. In all three of these cases—preaching, music, and liturgical symbols—we are drawn out of ourselves. We hear, see, touch and taste in ways that connect us to the saving power of Christ. At these moments hope arises and is nurtured by the possibility that God is doing something new in our lives and in the world. It is this hope that draws us out of the sanctuary to engage in acts of care, justice, and love.

20. One way of interpreting the downturn in young adults entering ordained ministry is that they were more fascinated with so-called worldly pursuits. But this only leads to other questions: Were they simply attracted to jobs with money and power? Or were they attracted by signs of God's unfolding glory outside of the institutional church?

21. Stringfellow, *A Private and Public Faith*, 56.

five

The Power to Transform the World

The Fifth Essential Component

*The church is a community affirming power
to transform individuals and society.*

The Church as an Agent of Transforming Power

WINTHROP HUDSON OFFERED THE intriguing proposal that new religious movements emphasized "the possibility of perfect sanctification, thus arousing a hunger for holiness and a life free from sin."[1] He used this idea to analyze divergent groups in nineteenth-century America. I want to borrow the idea to suggest that the church, from the very beginning, affirmed new life and strategies for change. These strategies are forms of grace which have power to transform individuals and society.

To speak in this way shatters the general impression that the practices of the church are only sacred rituals for worship or routine requirements for church order. There is no doubt that both views are present among the faithful. Some might even suggest a third option, that church practices are intended to resist any change. When these views predominate church life, the word *strategies* will probably only be used by a stewardship or social action committee. But what if the fundamental practices of the church

1. Hudson, *Religion in America*, 182.

are actually strategies for change? This would drastically alter the way we think of them. Take for example the baptism of infants. For many, such a practice is merely the official act of blessing and naming the new born child. But if one listens carefully (assuming the celebrant reads the full text), the original meaning is still there: baptism is a sign and seal of the child's incorporation into the Body of Christ. The parents, godparents, and congregation promise to nurture this child with the love of Christ. In fact, the parents and godparents are asked whether they renounce the evils of this world. (One can only wonder what evils they are prepared to renounce.) What we have at the heart of the baptism liturgy is the clear declaration that something is happening here that does in fact change things: The child is named as part of the community of Christ on earth and commitments are made by family, friends, and congregation to act in specific ways.[2] To strengthen this interpretation of baptism as a strategy for the Kingdom of God, consider the great commission where Jesus sends the disciples into the world to make disciples. How shall this be done? By baptism and teaching.

Baptism is not the only practice that might be called a strategy for changing the world. Consider the first words of Jesus in the Gospel of Mark: "The time is fulfilled and the Kingdom of God has come near; repent, and believe in the good news" (Mark 1:14). With these words Jesus invokes the traditions of the prophets calling the people back to the covenant by means of repentance and true faith. Following his example, the church has supported preachers in every age to proclaim the good news and call people to follow Jesus. Parallel to the role of preacher, Jesus also creates a new community by means of teaching. This includes his dramatic parables as well as the interpretations and applications of the law in the Sermon on the Mount. Just as the Mosaic Covenant provided structure to guide us in the ways of life, so Jesus makes it clear that if one wishes to be a disciple, one must keep his commandments.

---

2. To speak of baptism in this way does not condemn unbaptised infants to hell or remove them from the love of God. If the entire history of the covenants is based on love and grace, it is inconceivable that God's love is not extended to dying infants. But the fact that God loves all should not be used to negate the importance of being a part of the community of new life in Christ on earth. The point is that God wills a community on earth that participates in the new life of Jesus Christ. From this perspective, it does make a difference whether one participates in the new covenant, since we are speaking of the realization of new life on earth.

The idea that the church has access to transforming power, however, raises serious questions. The first is: What is the basis for such a claim? This goes to what is the very foundation of all Christian faith, namely, that God was in Christ redeeming the world. This affirmation of God's presence brings us again to the paradox we encountered in dealing with the question of authority: on the one hand, the church is derived from the incarnation of the Word in Jesus Christ, bringing new life; on the other hand it is not identical with Jesus Christ since it is still in the process of growing into the mind of Christ and still confesses its brokenness by the power of sin. Living in this paradox, the church witnesses to, and embodies, transforming grace. By grace God uses the fragile and sinful people of Christ to be witnesses and the bearers of the gift and promise.

In one sense, the issue here is really whether we are convinced God created the church as an agent of reconciliation. There is indeed a time for humility and a need to avoid false pretensions about our gifts and powers. But if we only do that we deny what God has done in Christ. The church must declare that Christ intended to create a covenant people to embody and demonstrate new life. If we expect nothing of the church, then that probably means that we still do not know the gifts of Christ. Why is it so strange to speak of the church as an agent of transforming power when we are quite at ease to speak of Scripture or the Lord's Supper in this way? In these two cases, God invests forms of this world with saving power. God does this not by external constraint but according to God's purpose. God creates forms of grace in this world without ceasing to be the sovereign God. Nor are these forms of grace magical powers that we can control or misuse. Our participation in forms of grace for the cause of Christ is legitimate only when we allow Christ to work through us.

The second question is the reverse of the first: how can one endorse such claims for the church when history shows so clearly that they have been abused? Time and again the church has pretended that it possesses the means of grace and will dispense or withhold grace only as it chooses. How easy it is for Protestants to lift up the inglorious case of the sale of indulgences in the sixteenth century as the attempt to use and control the forms of grace. But the real marketing of grace occurs every day in contemporary America when religion engages in competitive offers of saving power for personal gain or the defense of injustice. Against such arrogant claims regarding ecclesiastical power, believers must proclaim that it is

God who is changing the world, not the church. The church has access to, or possesses, the forms of grace only as a gift from God. By grace God chooses to use the church as a means of grace, and by grace God works in the world without the church. The moment we think that the church, or its leaders, possess the power to transform the world, we become yet another huckster trying to close a sale. The church does indeed have forms of grace capable of transforming people, but these are the gifts of Christ.

Finally, we need to deal with the question of means and ends. How can all the wonderful forms of grace be considered strategies for change without being devalued as merely means? Acts of love, prayers in worship, the celebration of the sacraments all have an inherent value and cannot be reduced merely to means toward some noble purpose. Worship and sacraments, teaching and fellowship, or the care of one another represent acts that are good in and of themselves. They are indeed demeaned if done for personal recognition, monetary gain, or because they are required by legalistic standards for ministry. Just as important, the church must protest against a world that so easily reduces people and things to means toward social, economic and political ends. There is indeed an inherent value to people, just as there is a value in fulfilling the ministries of the church. In what sense, therefore, may we speak of forms of grace as strategies? The answer lies in the fact that what we do is the way we participate in the fuller manifestation of the Kingdom of God on earth. The basic practices of the church are both ends (that is, signs of the coming of the Kingdom) and the means for changing ourselves and the world. The church already has received the gift of new life; it also is called to use these gifts to transform the world. What is unique about means and ends in the church, however, is that the means must always embody the goal. We must start out from where we want to be or we shall never get there. It is in this sense that the language of strategies is both an affirmation of the presence of Christ in what we say and do, as well as an affirmation that the church does not live for itself but for the Kingdom of God. The strategies embody as well as point to the goal which will be realized at the end of time. Thus it is not demeaning to say that baptism, preaching or the Lord's Supper are means of grace. That is precisely what happens when they are properly enacted. Ordinary life is interrupted, a divine Word is heard amid the noise of this world, and people are forced to make a choice for or against the Kingdom of God.

Having considered these three questions, we conclude with an affirmation. The church affirms that God is changing the world. On this we need to be clear: God, not the church, is changing the world. This testimony to God, however, draws the church into the transforming power of God in a twofold way: In the first place, the church is a witness to God's redemptive activity and lives in the hope that God will continue to bring forth new life. The church itself bears the marks of that transforming power and is itself a demonstration of the forms of grace. In the second place, the church is called to demonstrate how and why the forms of grace can transform the world in light of the Rule of God. The two affirmations flow from God's activity and the two require one another. Whenever the church fails to witness to what God is doing, it isolates itself from the very source of its life. Then all its claims to be a bearer of good news and new life lose their power. But if the church only speaks of God and fails to affirm that it participates in the transformation of the world, then it also loses credibility and power.

Patterns of Grace, Forms of the Church

Thus far I have suggested that God in Christ has given to the church gifts that embody grace and are the means or strategies to further the cause of Christ. Some of these gifts have been singled out and elevated to a high level of value, such as the sacraments and preaching. Lest we go too far in thinking that only some things are sacred, we need to be reminded that everything that sustains life and draws us into the circle of God's love is a form of grace. All food is a gift of God, not just sacramental bread and wine. Every act of care, kindness, or justice is a form of grace, not just the liturgical passing of the peace. But having said this, in the church's history there are specific things, acts and words which stand apart as forms of grace. In most cases they are mandated by Christ or associated with him. So the church relies on worship and sacraments, preaching and teaching, works of love and public witness as means for demonstrating saving power. In this sense, a sacrament or a sermon is a specific form of grace.

Individual forms of grace, however, seldom stand alone. Rather they are gathered together into broad patterns to celebrate and represent the grace of God to the world. When this happens, the individual acts retain their basic meaning but also become part of a larger system of faith and practice. For example, all Christians celebrate the Lord's Supper but consider how this basic act takes on different meanings when it appears in different traditions. The Lord's Supper comes to be shaped and invested with values derived from the distinctive character of the larger pattern. These larger patterns of grace represent identifiable ways to transform lives.

The idea that patterns of grace were distinct and had a unique role to play in the life of churches emerged during my study of atonement theories. When I started the study I expected to find a clear and direct correlation between a specific view of atonement and a specific denomination. But that did not happen. As a consequence, I was forced to examine what we call theories of atonement in a closer way. Upon further reflection, I was drawn to the conclusion that theories of atonement have two parts: first, an image of Jesus; second, a proposal as to how the benefits of Christ are shared with us. These two parts related to different questions. The images used to interpret Jesus (such as sacrifice, justifying grace, or wondrous love) answered the question: what actually happened in Jesus and why is it important? But having brought the listener or reader to this point, they posed a second question: How are the benefits of Christ communicated to believers across time and space? Was it by the sacraments, by faith, by works of love, or some other means? In effect, a theory of atonement is not complete until it answers both questions—as every preacher knows. Compare Acts 2:37, where Peter's sermon describing God's action in Jesus Christ prompts the listeners to ask: "What shall we do?"[3]

The realization that the good news of Christ is communicated in distinct ways brings us to the next stage of the analysis: Patterns of grace are the means for communicating the saving power of Jesus Christ. These patterns are often associated with specific images for interpreting Jesus: for example, the image of sacrifice is easily connected with the Eucharist, or the image of justifying grace is easily connected with proclamation and

---

3. This distinction between *what* Jesus does and *how* it is transmitted is implied in most writers. But not all are as explicit about it as was John Calvin, who first describes who Jesus is and what he does, followed by how we receive the grace of Christ. In Book Two of *The Institutes*, Calvin describes who Jesus is and what he does. In Book Three he turns to "The Way in Which We Receive the Grace of Christ . . . ," followed by Book Four, "The External Means or Aids by Which God Invites Us into the Society of Christ and holds us Therein." Cf. the Table of Contents in John Calvin, *The Institutes of the Christian Religion*, xi–xvii.

faith. But these connections are prompted more by historical association rather than logical necessity. Many writers speak of sacrifice to interpret Jesus but the means of communicating is not always the Lord's Supper. It could just as often be faith or acts of love and service. Consider the fact that many Christians use the imagery of penal substitution to interpret Christ (e.g., Roman Catholics, Presbyterians, and Mennonites), but see Christ's benefits being communicated in different ways. Conversely, a specific pattern can be connected to many images for Christ. If Anselm concludes his interpretation of Jesus by directing us to the sacraments, Abelard and Wesley see the sacraments as a sign of the wondrous love of God. Each pattern of grace can be employed by advocates of quite different interpretations of Jesus.

The more I worked with the distinction between the images for interpreting Jesus and the patterns of grace used to share the benefits of Christ, the following conclusion emerged: the actual form of churches was not determined so much by the images of Jesus as the way saving power is communicated to believers. This is the basis for the thesis, developed here and in the next chapter: the specific form of churches is determined by the way patterns of grace organize and give meaning to structures and practices of a church's life.

What then are these patterns that affect the formation of churches? From the list of ways apostolic is defined in the first chapter, I would propose six basic patterns of grace:

1. Sacramental participation in Christ. The emphasis here could fall upon baptism as dying and rising with Christ (Romans 5) or upon the Eucharist as participation in the new life in Christ by bread and wine. In either case, this pattern relies on worship and the spiritual life, supported by the authority of the ordained ministry, creeds and tradition of the church. The strength of this pattern is participation—daily and weekly—in the faith and life formed by baptism and Eucharist, which ties the community to the story of Jesus. When the sacraments are increased to seven (Roman Catholic), the sacraments come to provide a religious structure for all of life.

   Communities formed by this pattern run certain risks: the tendency for sacraments and rituals to become ends in themselves; the strong emphasis on religious orders and ordained ministry with authoritarian structures; the emphasis on sacred places and events can divide the realm of religion from what comes to be known as the secular world.

2. Proclamation of grace and faith as trust of the heart. Here we have the dual emphasis on proclamation of the good news and our response in faith, hope, and love. This pattern gathers together preaching, teaching (including the catechism and education for all ages), the study of Scripture, hymnody, and creeds as the means of proclamation. Strategies to nurture and strengthen faith have typically been an emphasis on vocation for all believers, study and prayer, congregational fellowship and care, and opportunities for service and witness. In the nineteenth century, two movements developed this pattern in new ways. In John Williamson Nevin and Philip Schaff, the Mercersburg theology urged that the Protestant emphasis on the proclaimed Word be enriched by a stronger tie to the sacraments and a recovery of the genuine Catholic heritage. In Horace Bushnell, the emphasis on proclamation and faith was connected to a broader understanding of nurture. From this perspective, nurture included preaching and teaching, but also all of the structures and practices of family and community life which form persons. In spite of their quite different settings (German Reformed and New England Congregationalism) these two traditions share the emphasis on the community as the way Christ is mediated to us as well as opposition to the individualism of nineteenth-century revivalism.

   The great strength of this pattern is the affirmation of God's sovereignty and the centrality of Jesus Christ, proclaimed as Lord and Savior, over against all worldly claims, even those of the institutional church. But the emphasis on faith as trust of the heart too easily becomes belief in the right things, i.e., doctrines or Bible. When this happens, absolute claims for doctrine or Bible produce a rigid authoritarian structure.

3. Rebirth in the Spirit. The dramatic references to the bestowal of the Spirit on Jesus and the church, as well as the need to be reborn in the Spirit, give this pattern its confidence that new life is transmitted by spiritual rebirth. While it does not necessarily shun creed, doctrine, or tradition, it is suspicious of claims to authority other than appeals to new life in the Spirit. Formal systems and practices may serve as

helpful guidelines, but they can never replace the authenticity born of the Spirit. Thus the emphasis usually falls upon the freedom of God to generate new forms of spiritual life, or to recapture a vision of the early church living by the power of the Spirit. The problems with this pattern emerge directly from its strength: to the extent that it shies away from tradition and structure, it appears disruptive. Without clear norms for testing the Spirit, it opens itself to extreme alternatives. It was for this reason that most traditions have insisted on a Christological test for claims to the Spirit: Is what you claim consistent with what we know of Jesus? The irony of this pattern, however, is that over time it usually does develop traditions and rules, often in quite strict form, which may be the occasion for new changes.

4. Participation in the new community of Christ. Any view of Christ's saving power which emphasizes the creation of a new, reconciled community on earth, is inevitably led to some form of this pattern: participation in a gathered community with its work (discipline), fellowship, witness, and service. One finds forms of this pattern in Roman Catholic orders, the Protestant gathered churches, and Anabaptist communities. One way of understanding millennial predictions for the coming of Christ is to see these as another form of participation in a community, defined in this case by expectation. The great strength is the creation of disciplined communities set apart from the world. In a surprising way, sometimes the distinctive life set apart from the world becomes a powerful witness to the world. To the extent that these communities live apart from the world, this pattern faces the problem of isolation. Likewise, the more communities seek to preserve their identity by rules and regulations, the more they run the risk of legalism, division, and loss of members.

5. Acts of love and justice. When Christ's saving power is perceived as new life in words and actions, then the pattern for transmitting the gospel will be engaging in works of love and justice. Drawing on the covenant tradition of the prophets and the teachings of Jesus, this pattern sees acts of love and justice as our faithful response to Christ and the means to change the world. This passion for demonstrating love and justice becomes the church's primary witness to the world.

We generally think of this pattern in terms of its liberal activist form, but it would be well to recognize that conservative Protestants have always made certain moral concerns a defining mark of faithfulness. Problems for this pattern arise in two ways: when absolute claims about goals and strategies are made, it inevitably isolates itself from others; when it ignores the traditional life and structures of the church, it runs the danger of cutting itself off from the religious sources of motivation and vision, which inspired it in the first place. If the first problem leads to claims of higher moral righteousness and legalism, the second problem tends to separate the movement from rank and file in the churches, even suggesting that religion has been reduced to morality.

6. Solidarity with Christ, who suffers with the oppressed. This pattern draws upon the New Testament affirmation that Jesus brings liberation to those who suffer and are oppressed. In its Roman Catholic expressions, this pattern draws together a very traditional view of Christ as the Incarnate Word with participation among the suffering in the struggles for justice and freedom. But it has faced tremendous resistance from traditional Catholics because of its alliance with political and economic strategies in the name of Christ. Among American Protestants, the pattern appears in Black Churches as well as feminist, peace, and environmental movements, but in quite different forms. The strength of these efforts is the insistence that Jesus must be redefined as the source of justice for the oppressed. They face the challenge of simultaneously offering major critiques of traditional theology and practice while affirming constructive alternatives. This has been a work in progress over the last fifty years and there have been great gains as well as great divisions within churches on these issues.

As we consider these patterns of grace, several comments are in order. First, while the liberal activist and liberationist patterns have much in common, they are quite different in history and theological approach. In American Protestantism, the liberal activist pattern goes back several centuries, drawing upon numerous attempts to define the essence of Jesus as his teachings of love. In the nineteenth century it found expression in movements which subordinated doctrinal differences to practical, moral goals (e.g., abolition and temperance). In the twentieth century it was expressed in the Social Gospel. The great movements of the last 60 years focused on rallying people for social action, based primarily on the moral imperatives of the gospel. In many ways it is the dominant pattern of church leaders at the national level (e.g., among mainline churches, the United Church of Christ would be the best example). The Liberationist pattern, in its Roman Catholic form, has combined orthodox doctrine with engagement for justice among the poor because that is where Christ is. Black and feminist theologies—while quite different—are closer to the liberationist pattern, rather than the liberal activist pattern, because so much criticism is directed against the church as the defender of the status quo. To the extent that the activist pattern wants to apply the church's social teachings, the liberationist pattern tends to step back from the church to begin again in solidarity with Jesus among all who suffer.

Second, we need to be reminded that these patterns are constellations of specific structures and practices which mediate grace, held together by a central conviction regarding the transmission of saving power. The fact that certain things (Scripture, creed, sacrament, preaching, or teaching) appear in all of them does not negate the differences between the patterns. It simply emphasizes how each pattern approaches these specific acts in different ways and uses them for different purposes. For example, high liturgical traditions still include the sermon but it is often reduced to a shorter version called a homily; conversely, most Protestants emphasize preaching but still celebrate the Eucharist once a month or four times a year.

Third, while particular churches are organized by a dominant pattern, the other patterns are also present in some form. Call to mind the typical Roman Catholic, Presbyterian, and Mennonite congregation. They look and act very differently. Each appears to be marked by one or more of the patterns. But each still contains all the remaining patterns. The Roman Catholics still value proclamation, rebirth in the Spirit, the church as gathered community (e.g., the parish and monastery), acts of love and justice, as well as liberationist themes. The same can be said for Presbyterians and Mennonites, though the former would probably give prominence to proclamation/faith and the latter to a combination of the disciplined community and acts of love. The point is this: one pattern, or some combination of patterns, is what gives specific churches their characteristic form as a community of Christ. But the dominant pattern does not negate or deny the others. In fact, if this were to occur, it would produce a very constricted and narrow form of church life. Not only would it be theologically questionable, it could hardly sustain itself over time.

Fourth, just as these patterns give form and substance to particular traditions, they also become sources of tension between traditions. We come to love our own traditions, but also fear and dislike other traditions. In fact, we tend to argue for our preferred mode of transmission by arguing against the weaknesses and/or corruptions of other patterns. Thus Roman Catholics point to the splintering of Protestant churches, while minimizing the problems of an authoritarian structure. But Protestants have no difficulty doing just the reverse: pointing to abuses of authority and power while minimizing the proliferation of divisions. In an ecumenical age it will be difficult to relate to other traditions unless we can set aside our negative stereotypes of alternative forms of grace. Of course, this is already happening as Christians interact across old boundaries.

Fifth, the tensions between the patterns are not just between churches, but within each denomination and each congregation. That is, each mainline Protestant church is internally divided by appeals to reform the church according to different patterns of grace: sacraments, preaching, spiritual rebirth, social witness, and acts of love. This produces a situation where some feel under attack for holding to the traditional pattern and others see themselves as agents of change. For example, when traditional Catholics or Protestants find someone arguing for a liberal activist or liberationist form of the church, the debate can easily divide the community. The same can be said when forms and practices associated with spiritual rebirth appear in Catholic or mainline Protestant communities. Perhaps the most common point of conflict over these patterns is the call or appointment of a new pastor. This easily becomes the occasion for vigorous debate over the form of the church, as opposing forms are represented by members of the search committee and candidates. For this reason both sides need to state honestly their commitments regarding patterns of grace. Does this mean a congregation cannot change by incorporating aspects of other forms of grace? Not at all. The other patterns are already present in the congregation's current life, though probably receiving minimal attention. They certainly are present in the congregation's history and authoritative documents. Shifting attention from one pattern to another is not revolutionary in the sense of introducing foreign or new ideas. It does, however, involve a change in mindset and practice (e.g., proposals to have the Eucharist every Sunday). But such changes need to be made through a process of open discussion, prayer, and study with reference to the total life of the congregation. They do not occur by a new pastor or a committee imposing new structures and practices.

Finally, while the six patterns are the distinctive marks of separate traditions, the good news is that each points to a valid way of communicating the saving power of Christ. They are exclusive or divisive only when we insist that one is the only valid means of grace. What is so unusual about this tendency for claiming only one pattern is the fact that everyone still incorporates some aspect of the other pattern in their faith and life. What has happened in this ecumenical age is that God is mixing things up more and more, as we discover that we can indeed incorporate not only the specific acts and symbols of other patterns, but the larger values as well.

Patterns of Grace: The Key to Our Past and Future

Let us begin by affirming the importance of patterns of grace. As the primary agent in the formation of churches, patterns of grace are crucial for two reasons:

First, they open the way for understanding in positive terms why churches or traditions differ. We no longer need to resort to describing alternative patterns from our own as wrong or irrelevant. Since each affirms a valid means of communicating the grace of God, there is no need to defend my traditional preference by denouncing the alternatives. Their differences point to the richness in the gifts of grace God has entrusted to churches. What this means, then, is that churches have a way of living with one another in peace, honoring the different traditions while at the same time affirming the gifts which God has given to each.

Second, the patterns provide us with the key for living in the new world of mutual exchange among ecumenical churches. It is true that we have treated them as mutually exclusive and too often denounced alternative patterns in the attempt to maintain our sense of faithfulness. But careful analysis shows us quite clearly that they are different but not mutually exclusive. What they do reveal is that Christian faith and practice are much richer than we ever imagined and that when one pattern cuts itself off from the others, it will deprive itself of being enriched by the fullness of Christ. The fact is that the age of mutual interchange began nearly a century ago, or more. The laity already live in such a world—perhaps more so than religious leaders—by virtue of inter-marriage, neighborhood associations, work, and public schools. Most mainline churches have also moved into such a world, by virtue of multiple forms of sharing.

If patterns of grace are so important, what prevents us from a genuine embrace of new forms of life together? The problem is that even as pilgrims on the way, we carry excess baggage. Here we need to reflect on two issues which make the embrace difficult. One is the relation of justification and sanctification; the other is the relation of the church gathered and the church scattered (i.e., the beloved community joined by grace and the community scattered in witness, service, and protest in the world). These two polarities weigh heavy upon those trying to be more inclusive. Let me explain.

On the first issue, everyone nods general assent to the unity of justification and sanctification. But in reality communities lean one way or the other, partly out of conviction and partly as a reaction to the dangers they perceive in the other direction. This leads to a separation of the religion of grace and the religion of power. The religion of grace affirms God's gracious acceptance of sinners. It is cautious about perfectionist and utopian dreams because of the pervasiveness of sin. This produces the rhythm of confession of sin and the announcement of forgiveness, endlessly repeating itself. Critics call it cheap grace or even a paralysis of the human spirit: one is forever mindful of sin but unwilling or unable to risk a move toward change. It is captured so well by Augustine's ambivalence, earnestly desiring transformation, but not now. By contrast, the religion of power affirms that God is changing things now. It expects something of God and declares that God expects something of us this very day. Many of the people attracted to this message are powerless and see the religion of grace as far too comfortable with the status quo. For them, the religion of power is an example of God's intervention in this world to raise up the poor and neglected. Yet the religion of power has also had great success among middle and upper classes, translated into a message of self-help. In this form it has become a major part of American Cultural Religion, believing that God exists primarily to provide for our needs. What concerns the critics of the religion of power is the optimism that we can cross over from sin to perfection, or attempt to assure continual progress by stricter adherence to rules. Whether the result is naïve optimism or self-righteous legalism, in either case the religion of power easily reaches too far. In its popular forms, the danger of over-extension finds expression in the declarations that God will bless the faithful with perfect health and an abundance of material things.

So how do justification and sanctification, or grace and power, relate to the six patterns? In general, the first two patterns gravitate toward justifying grace while the latter four move toward expectations of new life. As noted above, when traditions separate grace and power, each side suffers a specific set of ailments. Such analysis is helpful, but I am not sure we can think our way out of this polarization. As will be argued later, the more likely solution lies in the direction of returning to our origin in God's gift and promise, as well as the mutual interchange between people on each side of this polarity.

The second issue has also been a divisive one for communities. The church gathers to celebrate its origin in Christ. It also gathers as a sign of God's intention: to be a community reconciled to God and one another. It is not an exaggeration to say that the first thing the church must do is to be the church: a community of worship, faith, fellowship, and service. The church cannot be a light to the world unless it first lives in the light of Christ. But an equally compelling case can be made for the church scattered into the world. God's goal can never be defined simply as the creation of the church set apart, but as the salvation of the world and the unfolding of God's glory in the world. The disciples are commissioned to go into the world—the very world created and loved by God—that all may believe and love. Gathering may have logical and temporal priority, but going out into the world is the only way the church may fulfill its calling to be the light of the world.

It is difficult to name the reasons why some communities see the church gathered or scattered as the decisive moment. In quite different ways, the first four patterns of grace give priority to the church gathered. In the first and second (Sacramental Participation and Proclamation of the Word) the gathered community is the place where the Christian life begins and is nurtured. In the third and fourth (Rebirth in the Spirit and the Gathered Community) the same may be said, but there is a stronger sense of being called out of the world and set apart from the world. If the first two separate themselves from the world by the sheer force of the institutional structures created, the second two separate themselves by intentional design. This is especially the case in monastic movements, Anabaptist communities and free churches marked by the quest for holiness.

The tendencies for separation among these groups, however, are balanced by all sorts of ministries of evangelism, teaching, medical care, and social service. We must remember that medieval monasteries were not only set apart but also existed to serve dioceses through evangelism and teaching, and to reform the church. The same may be said of Anabaptist churches which stand out because of their courageous witness to forgiveness and peace. The last two patterns (Acts of Love and Justice and Solidarity with Christ) give priority to witness and service in the world. Whether they see themselves being sent by the gathered church or going into the world to be in solidarity with Christ, those living out these patterns do maintain some connection with the gathered church. But they believe that the gathered church was created so that Christians might engage the world in the name of Christ.

While it may not be clear why communities give priority to the church gathered or scattered, it is clear what happens when the two poles are cut off from one another. The church that is only gathered suffers from isolation and is prone to resist all change. So much of mainline Protestantism has struggled with this development, seeking to preserve the sanctity of the beloved community from external threat. Mainline Protestant congregations easily become preoccupied with nurturing the beloved community as the ultimate goal. It is the temptation the disciples felt when witnessing the transfiguration of Jesus on the mountain: they wanted to stay there. But the more churches resist active engagement with the world, the more they freeze themselves in time. Failing to deal with scientific, moral, or social issues too often leads to a code of silence regarding crucial issues. Since they failed to deal with new ideas (e.g., regarding the Bible) or difficult social issues (e.g., race, women, or sex) they became victims of their own deferred spiritual maintenance. Fearing that Christ could not handle difficult issues, they reached the point where crucial issues could not be discussed in church. Time and again so many Protestant churches were unprepared for crises in the world. To be sure, in the past half-century many liberal and conservative Protestants have aligned themselves on one side or the other of the great social issues. But if we look at the Culture Wars over this period, one must ask whether they were engaging the world with the gospel or simply allying their churches with liberal and conservative movements in the culture. A reoccurring theme in American religious history is the tendency of conservative communities to isolate themselves from the world. They wish to preserve the purity of faith by standing against the world. That this pits them against many other Christians or creates a terrible choice for their children are consequences they seem willing to accept.

By contrast, when the church is only scattered, it suffers the risk of being cut off from the traditions and practices that nourish faith. It is very difficult for movements of love and justice to maintain their mission without the discipline of larger communities and the renewal of the Spirit. In the last half-century, the liberal activist pattern has found strong expression in mainline leadership positions as well as movements outside of the church (e.g., movements dealing with race, peace, and women). In both cases, defining the church solely in terms of acts of love and justice has faced two problems.

The first is that it tends to assume that American churches are already committed to change in the name of justice. It was as if we all knew what we should do but only forgot. Thus activist leaders tend to be stronger on the moral imperative without spending much time on the transformation of hearts and minds. To their surprise, church members were slow to respond to the imperative. Take for example, the civil rights movement in the 1950s and 1960s. Why were white Protestants shocked to find some pastors, priests, nuns, and rabbis marching in the streets? The reason was that they had never connected their decision for Jesus and church membership with justice for black people. It was never part of the agreement. The same problem reappeared on most of the other social debates which followed. In other words, before we can mobilize churches and members for causes of justice, we need to deal with the primary question of God's act in Jesus Christ. But when activist movements in and outside of the church cut themselves off from the practices of worship, education, fellowship, and ministry of the gathered church, they distance themselves from the true motivation for action, namely, the transforming grace of Jesus Christ.

The second problem is the inability to maintain the vision of love and justice without the Word of judgment and grace as mediated by the traditional communities. The Christian life is not self-renewing, as if it were a power system first charged at baptism, confirmation, or some decisive moment in young adulthood. It is a daily struggle between sin and grace, between the temptations of ruling over others and the call to servanthood. Ministries of service and witness must constantly be renewed by the hearing of the Word and receiving bread and wine, by prayer and reflection, by the fellowship and support of larger communities. Likewise, movements and institutions committed to acts of love and justice need a similar kind of review and renewal by interaction with other patterns of grace. Both the church gathered and scattered need one another and both need the renewal by the gospel.

Here it is also appropriate to refer to another form of the church scattered in American society. This is the number of people, once connected to the church, who now live their lives separated from institutional religion. Some have been pushed out by oppressive practices of churches. Some are alienated because of disagreements. But all have adopted to some degree the American creed that the individual is the basic unit of religion. They choose what to believe and not to participate in organized religion. Since most still seem to acknowledge some link to faith in God and/or the values of love and justice, they constitute a new form of the church scattered. They, most of all, suffer the risk of not knowing what Christian faith is about because their only religious education came in childhood. And they are cut off from being sustained by a community of acceptance and care. They are reluctant to speak of religious needs, though they are often concerned about issues of identity, acceptance, guilt, or purpose. To the extent that they are isolated from religious traditions, they are unable to consider these matters in religious language and are less and less able to hand down to their children a religious life.

How easy it is to affirm on paper that justification and sanctification belong together, or that the church must be gathered and scattered. To date we have had little success trying to talk ourselves out of our divisions into a more inclusive way of life. But hope does appear when communities pursue a vision of the new life, which both precedes and transcends these divisions. In such cases, the power of the gospel shatters the limits we place upon the church.

For example, consider the affirmation of reconciliation, so basic to the gospel. Here is the theme of forgiveness, or justification, which creates the church. The church gathers to remember and be renewed by the power of God's forgiveness. But in fact, it does not end there. Jesus commands us to forgive one another. In The Lord's prayer, we request God to "forgive us our sins, as we forgive one another." Numerous passages in the New Testament affirm the expectation that those who are loved by God will love others: for example, the good tree bears good fruit. The point is this: notice how the reality of forgiveness bestowed on the individual generates the drive toward being a forgiving person. In other words, to receive grace naturally leads to the power of being graceful. Here there is no separation of justification and sanctification.

A striking illustration of this is the practice of forgiveness among the Amish. For the Amish, the church is set apart from the world by believers' baptism, adherence to the Sermon on the Mount, and non-resistance. Jesus' command to be reconciled to one another in Matthew 18 is implemented in worship twice a year. Thus they live out how God's forgiveness generates movement toward being a forgiving person. But here we come to a surprising paradox: on the one hand, these practices set the Amish apart from the world in a gathered community that has a certain monastic character; on the other hand, at crucial moments they are forced to interact with the world. Let me explain. In 1993 a man driving on a rural road in Ohio killed several Amish children. It was reported that he was unrepentant. In 2005 a man killed five Amish children in their school at Nichol Mines, in Lancaster, Pennsylvania. In the first case the Amish leaders indicated how difficult it was to forgive the driver, especially since he showed no remorse, but indicated that they would forgive him. In the second case, Amish elders went to the widow and parents of the killer and expressed forgiveness. Both stories were covered widely in the news; in fact, the second case became a world wide media event. People were astounded by the absence of anger or a desire for revenge. In both cases, the cloistered community suddenly was a public community. The practice of forgiveness was extended to outsiders who had committed violence against them. In other words, against the conventional expectation, a tradition normally defined as a gathered community became the most visible public witness for the love of Christ.

Now let us extend the analysis in a different direction. Among the Amish the insistence of forgiveness is the defining mark of the church. But consider Martin Luther's view of the church. In his *Large Catechism*, Luther declares that we are brought to the church by the Holy Spirit, enabling us to receive all of Christ's gifts. The two primary gifts are: forgiveness and the resurrection to eternal life. Luther goes on to say that the church is the community of believers made holy by the Spirit working in us through forgiveness. The Christian life is one of daily growth by the power of the Spirit, even though we never reach perfection until our death. Then in a later essay on the church, Luther lists the seven signs of the church. After preaching the Word, baptism and Eucharist, the fourth sign is the power of the keys based on Matthew 18: that Christians are to repent their sins and forgive one another—or be excluded from the community.[4] Now it is true that Luther also saw the church alongside of the state, both ordained by God, maintained infant baptism and condoned the state's violence against the Anabaptists. In these ways he differed from the Anabaptists. But for the moment, consider carefully what Luther is saying about the church as church: It is formed by Word and sacrament through the power of the Spirit as a community of forgiveness, which is to grow in love toward one another. If this is the case, there can be no resting in justification, no taking comfort in endless announcements of grace without the awakening of graceful hearts.

Two questions are prompted by this convergence on the church between the Anabaptists and Luther. The first is for Lutherans and Reformed: Why have we not lived out this vision of the church as a community of forgiveness? Let us put the question in a bold way: What would have happened if the children at Nichol Mines were killed in a Lutheran or Presbyterian Church? Would there be any expectation of a forgiving response? The second question is: Does the similarity between Luther and the Anabaptists regarding the inner life of the church create an opportunity for a new understanding between groups that for centuries have lived quite separately? If Jesus calls all Christians to practice forgiveness inside and outside of the church, does this not break down the walls we have constructed between justification and sanctification, the church gathered and scattered?

4. Cf. *The Large Catechism of Martin Luther*, 59–64; and "On the Councils and the Church, (1539)," 3–178.

Time has been given to the polarities of justification and sanctification, and the church gathered and scattered, because these issues too often prevent communities from moving out of their preferred pattern of grace. How then shall we create a desire to think about the church in new ways? We can catalogue the weaknesses derived from living only in one pattern of grace, but these are already well known. What will give us leverage to dislodge long standing preferences for one pattern and fears of the others? While exposing the imbalances and excesses of single mindedness may attract some attention, the weaknesses of each pattern are already well known. Change is more likely to occur by a vision of new life, rather than criticism of what is. The more effective way to dislodge the log jam is to return to the church's point of origin: the primacy of God's grace and the intervention of holiness for the redemption of the world. If this is the goal for the coming of Jesus Christ, then we are allowed (dare one say required) to think in new ways about the church. This vision cannot be captured only by the grace of justification or the grace of sanctification; nor can it be embodied only as a gathered people or as a scattered people of God. As we grow uncomfortable with confining the church to one side of these polarities, so we also lose zeal for thinking that one pattern of grace captures the fullness of this vision by itself. But each of the six patterns does have a place in describing strategies for change and the form of the church. Consider these remarks as an expression of how we are moving to combine the six patterns:

- From the standpoint of the goal of God's intervention in Jesus Christ, it is inconceivable that it could be realized without communities of faith gathered together by the grace of sacraments and the proclamation of the good news.

- On their better days, Christians have affirmed that sacramental acts, the reading of Scripture and the proclaimed word are nothing without the power of the Holy Spirit opening our eyes and ears so that we might receive new life. From this point of view it has always been an overstatement to suggest that anything works automatically by the mere doing of it, be it the Lord's Supper or reading Scripture.

- To take another step, receiving the sacrament, the proclaimed Word and the Spirit have always drawn believers into a community of faith, hope, and love. The individualism of American culture may be understandable, but it denies the whole point of the new life Jesus bestows upon his followers. God's goal includes communities of new life on earth.

- Finally, if the goal is the revealing of God's glory to the ends of the earth, then communities of Jesus Christ must engage in witness, service, and love in the world. Whether they are compelled by the love of Christ or seek to be in solidarity with Christ who is with all who suffer—this distinction cannot be a stumbling block. Preaching, teaching, evangelism, witness, protest, service, and care are to be practiced in the world.

By keeping our eye on the primacy of God's goal for the intervention of Christ, a much more inclusive vision of the Christian life emerges. On the one hand, this opens the way for greater integration of the six patterns. The natural connections between proclamation, sacraments, and spiritual renewal with the community of disciples active in the world become evident. The more we think and work with all of the patterns in mind, the more they cease to be opposites or conflicting alternatives.[5] On the other hand, it is helpful to be mindful of the tensions between the six patterns and not pretend that they are completely resolved. Given our tendencies toward personal preferences and single mindedness, even the best efforts will still face problems of excess in one or more directions. There is something quite striking about each of the six patterns. Each in its own way points to an aspect of the new life which must be affirmed. Knowing our history, we need these affirmations as words of judgment and grace.

We began the chapter with the proposal that the church is a community that claims transforming power. This prompted a consideration of how most of the structures and practices of churches do in fact function as strategies to change individuals and the world. We then observed how these distinct acts and symbols are gathered together in patterns of grace. Drawing on the way theories of atonement appear in theology and

---

5. A graceful memory I have from my time at Lancaster Seminary was when Mennonite students asked whether they could use the chapel on Sunday night to celebrate the Lord's Supper. The chapel is loaded with images from the Bible, images of Catholic and Protestant saints, surrounded by Victorian-Romanesque architecture. After years of worshiping on Wednesday morning with an ecumenical gathering of students and faculty, these students chose to worship in a new way as Mennonites.

preaching, we saw how these patterns of grace are the ways the saving power of Christ is communicated to us over time and space. Finally it was proposed that these patterns of grace determine the form of church life and practice. This leads us to the next chapter, where our attention turns to the church as the community of Christ, which embodies new life in its structures and practices.

six

The Community of Christ

THE FINAL CHAPTER IS organized around the three themes announced at the beginning. The first section introduces the sixth essential component, namely, the church as the community of Christ. This meets the goal of providing a more inclusive definition of the church.

The second section continues the discussion of how specific traditions are formed by patterns of grace. This provides a positive theory to explain why Christians differ, allowing us to honor the variety of ways Christians claim faith, structures, and practices.

The third section will make a case for an ecumenical or inclusive form of the church. As suggested at the outset, this can be done while still honoring the variety of traditions present among Christians.

Treasure in Earthen Vessels

The sixth essential component of the church:

The church is a community which embodies in structures and practices the new life of Christ and the Spirit:

- *worship, sacraments, and spiritual life;*
- *music, art, and symbols;*
- *proclamation within and outside the community;*
- *creeds, catechism, and teachings;*

- *education at all stages of life;*
- *call and nurture of leaders;*
- *marriage, family, and inter-generational life;*
- *fellowship and care of one another;*
- *service and witness, in and outside the church;*
- *stewardship;*
- *physical presence in the world (architecture);*
- *governance which orders the life of the church and sets it apart from the world;*
- *ecumenical relations among Christians and other religious groups.*

We may now develop what was emphasized at the beginning, namely, that the church is a social community, tied to its past and future. As such the church is an inter-generational community in larger cultural settings. From the beginning it had to deal with internal and external needs. On the one hand it had to determine what members believe, how it shall worship, pray and sing, nurture children, work to sustain the community, and relate to the world outside the church. On the other hand, it has always been compelled to distinguish itself from those who do not believe, protect itself from threats and decide how it would engage in witness and service in the world.

Given these challenges, it should not surprise us that churches depend on structures and practices. Let us note at the outset that the things listed above are stated in generic terms (e.g., Christian worship). At this level of the discussion we do not specify how they do it, who is authorized, or where it may take place. The list consists of things churches do in order to exist in this world—not just to survive—but to be faithful to Jesus Christ and the hope of the coming of the Kingdom of God. As such these structures and practices are necessary for the church. To defend this claim we need to say more about how they function.

Church structures and practices are of mixed origin; they vary in form and function. Some were inherited from Judaism (e.g., forms of worship, teachings such as the Decalogue and Sacred Writings), while others were mandated by Christ (e.g., two sacraments and teachings). Some are derived from the church's origin in Christ and the Spirit (e.g., the Sabbath as the Day of Resurrection, prayers, a church calendar retelling the story of Jesus, the New Testament and creeds). Then there are many things borrowed from contemporary cultures and/or created by churches, such as music, architecture, and governance. One can easily connect some of these with the internal needs of churches, while others speak to the issue of the relation to the outside world. Others are ways to organize and value time, for example, the Sabbath, practices relating to Advent, Christmas, Lent, and Holy Week; others organize space, such as churches, cathedrals, monasteries, schools, hospitals, and institutions of mercy. Some are community practices while others relate to the individual and/or family life. With the exception of celibate monastic communities, I cannot think of a Christian community enduring over time which does not include these elements in some way. They are the ways community life is ordered, sustained and nourished.

But even this requires further explanation. The structures and practices are necessary not simply because they are commonly used, but because they embody the new life of Jesus Christ. We need to hear both sides of Paul's affirmation in 2 Corinthians 4:7: "But we have this treasure in clay jars, so that it may be made clear that this extraordinary power belongs to God and does not come from us." Protestants have made much of this verse, refusing to allow things of this world to be invested with too much authority or power. Our structures and practices are finite, earthen vessels. In a world filled with tyrants who do in fact claim too much, as well as religious leaders who do the same, such a warning is always appropriate. But we also need to hear the other side of Paul's affirmation: in these earthen vessels there actually is a treasure. As difficult as it may seem, and against all our disbelief and worldly cynicism, the new life of Christ is poured into the structures and practices of the church. This is why the structures and practices that embody new life must be included in the definition of the church.

There are many structures and practices for two reasons. On the one hand they relate to the many forms of grace. In the earlier study of theories of atonement, I argued that saving power takes many forms as grace is directed toward multiple human needs as well as God's purposes. There really is a difference between forgiveness of sin for the individual troubled heart and the reconciliation of divided parties. Likewise, liberation is not the same as forgiveness. Liberation speaks to matters of freedom from compulsive behavior and suffering caused by oppressive forces which we do not control. But even an extended catalogue of human needs cannot describe saving power without reference to how God is ultimately renewing and restoring the creation according to the divine purposes. In other words, we need a variety of structures and practices to express the many aspects of the new life Jesus brings.

On the other hand, the variety of structures and practices reflects the rich and multi-layered dynamics of community life. It is a community that worships, sings, shares fellowship and resources, teaches, bears witness, and orders its life by faith, love, and hope. But it is also a community that attends to the life cycle of individuals and families, to weddings and the birth of children, to the sick and dying, the four seasons as well as the seasons of the church year.

The distinction between forms of saving power and the dynamics of community life, however, should not be taken to infer that some of the structures and practices relate solely to the so-called spiritual realm and others solely to life on earth. Christian faith has always rejected such a split, affirming that the Kingdom of God has come to earth, that the very structures and practices of daily human life are redeemed and elevated to a new level. For example, whether one considers marriage a sacrament or a rite of the church, in either case it points to love as a gift of grace.

The link between the structures and practices of the community and the new life of Christ explains why they come to have so much value, why they are so hard to change, and why they cause so many quarrels. These things have value because they are the ways in which the new life is transmitted, nourished and sustained. For this reason they acquire religious value. They are not disconnected or unrelated from the so-called substantial matters named in the creed. Each element, small or large, is linked to the norms which govern faith and life. They express a community's identity and formation in Christ, claims to authority, strategies for transforming persons and society, and a vision of the goal of history. For those who value them as such, they are not secondary but become marks of genuine faith. It is quite natural and inevitable for structures and practices which are bearers of new life to acquire special status, since they function as means of grace. One can even argue that it is a good thing: God intends the church to be a community on earth, continuing over time through generations, demonstrating the new life, and witnessing to the world.

But remember the obvious: All Christians do not pour the treasure into the same vessels, or, even when they do, it is not done in exactly the same way. The process occurs in such a way that congregations and traditions give special meaning to the structures and practices. Illustrations are readily at hand. All Christians worship, pray, sing, and read Scripture. But who shall lead worship, or when and how Christians worship is governed by the normative understanding of each tradition. The worship practices will also reflect the way churches understand authority, ways to change individuals and society, and the vision of the future. The same may be said for the way Christians pray and sing. Shall prayers be confined to written traditions, read by those authorized by the church, or shall they be spontaneous, with each member contributing as led by the Spirit? Even in this ecumenical age, visits to different churches reveal fairly clear differences in musical traditions and hymns. Not everyone hears a choir sing medieval plainsong, or chants a psalm, or sings "A Mighty Fortress is Our God," or "Precious Lord." Finally, who shall select passages of Scripture to be read and who shall interpret them? The way churches answer these questions says a great deal about their general understanding of Christianity as well authority and tradition. The point is that the primary way our deepest commitments and values are actually present in churches is through the community's structures and practices. Lutheran students of theology may read Luther's treatises or Commentary on Romans, but Lutherans sing "A Mighty Fortress is Our God." A small number of Calvinists have ever read Calvin, but most of those confirmed know the answer to the question: "What is my only comfort in life and in death?" To this first question *The Heidelberg Catechism* declares: "That I belong, both body and soul and in life and in death, not to myself, but to my faithful savior Jesus Christ . . ."
[1] Few have read Moltmann's powerful revival of the eschatological vision for the contemporary church, but all have prayed: "Thy Kingdom come, thy will be done, on earth as it is in heaven."

We must acknowledge, however, that the positive assessment of structures and practices creates problems for Protestants. The problem is not that we have been reluctant to embrace things of this world. We have done that in small and large ways, some for good and others for evil. Rather, the problem I have in mind is that our official theology does not equip us very well for understanding or nurturing the positive struc-

1. *The Heidelberg Catechism: A New Translation for the 21st Century*, 29.

tures and practices needed to support the community. As H. Richard Niebuhr argued in *The Kingdom of God in America*, a theology based on the sovereignty of God and the limitations of all individual or communal claims makes it difficult to create, to embrace, or to honor things which express and support the community.[2] To be sure, Luther declared that the treasure of the church—the only treasure—is the gospel. Calvin makes a similar claim at the beginning of Book IV of the *Institutes*.[3] He even goes so far to say that if God is our Father, the church is our mother and that we are rightfully under her care until we "mature and at last reach the goal of faith."[4] Nevertheless, Calvin displays an undercurrent of caution in the way he speaks of the church. Instead of focusing on the way the community of Christ elevates us to a higher form of being, time and again he speaks of the church as necessary because of human frailty. For example, because of our ignorance and sloth, God provides for physical forms in this world to deal with our weakness.[5] So teachers are established because of our weakness.[6] In effect, the general framework for speaking of the structures and practices of the church is God's willingness to accommodate the gospel to our capacity.[7] When applied to the sacraments, he notes that it is because of our ignorance and dullness that these signs are given "to establish us in faith."[8] In the same passage he continues: God "so tempers himself to our capacity that, since we are creatures who always creep on the ground, cleave to the flesh, and do not think about or even conceive of anything spiritual, he condescends to lead us to himself even by these earthly elements, and to set before us in the flesh a mirror of spiritual blessings." To be sure, in all these passages, Calvin emphasizes that this divine condescension attests to the mercy of God who is mindful of our need. But the motive does not remove the negative stigma regarding church structures and practices. In fact, in the very next sentence he contemplates that if we were incorporeal (i.e., spiritual beings) we would receive the message without physical signs. Is the implication that it would

2. Cf. especially Ch. 2, Niebuhr, H. R., *The Kingdom of God in America*, 45–87.

3. Calvin, *Institutes*, 1012.

4. Ibid.

5. Ibid., 1011.

6. Ibid., 1018.

7. Ibid., 1012.

8. Ibid., 1278.

be better if we did not need these things? Would it be preferable not to be together in communities on earth with spiritual and physical needs?

If there is caution in Calvin, there is outright suspicion in Zwingli. In his reform of the great church in Zurich, all statues, pictures, and symbols were removed, the murals were covered with paint, and the church was left with a communion table, baptismal font and a lectern holding the Bible. One is overwhelmed by the starkness of the sanctuary and the emphasis on the invisible spoken Word. Luther may have initiated a movement dependent upon the written and spoken word, but his reform did not go to the extent of the Reformed tradition, or for that matter, the Anabaptists and English Independents. If these examples do not give us pause, consider the portrayal of marriage in the older version of the Book of Common Prayer. We are commanded to marry in order to procreate and to limit the lust of the flesh. The implication appears to be that since men are out of control, the solution is to lock them up in marriage in the hope that they will restrict their passions to one woman. This is hardly a positive affirmation of life together in marriage.

These reminders of the theology of major parts of Protestantism reveal a serious ambivalence regarding ecclesial structures and practices. One may well wonder whether the preference for defining the church in terms of several articles of faith as the essentials (i.e., our origin and life in Christ, with everything else being secondary), reflects this caution and suspicion toward earthly things. By contrast, if we are going to affirm the church as a social community in time and space, then we need to embrace the structures and practices that support it. Such an embrace means that we need to move beyond caution to a positive affirmation of the new life in Christ. Dare we say that the life of the community in Christ transforms human existence? Such a claim has risks, given our Protestant protest against the medieval claim that religious orders were a higher level of religious life, above the laity. But here we are speaking of all those united in Christ by baptism and Eucharist, not just a few elevated to religious orders. Nor does the claim imply an attempt to transcend finite life, but just the opposite: it is the affirmation of our life together on earth. The structures and practices which embody the new life include Word and Sacrament, to be sure, but they also include music, architecture, the use of money, art, governance, friendship, love and marriage, and the care of all ages.

The rationale for this affirmation of real community life is twofold: it rests on an appeal to the goodness of creation. We are made for life together. Friendship is a higher form of human existence than solitary life. Love and marriage open us to a richer form of humanity. It is most striking that in Genesis 2, God is not offended by the love shared between the man and the woman. We are not commanded to love only God, but to love all things in God and God above all things. This does not mean that everyone must marry or, if they do, have large families. Rather it affirms that we become fully human in the intimacy of self-revelation within friendship, family, and social relations. The affirmation also depends on an appeal to the incarnation. The incarnation is not a momentary flash and clap of thunder, but the presence of the risen Christ and the Holy Spirit in the church—not just in our so-called spiritual moments of prayer, preaching, or reading Scripture. How quickly we forget that it was in the breaking of bread that the eyes of the disciples were opened or that with bread and wine we are joined with him and with one another. To make the point with another simple example, the church is not a weekend campout. It is the historic community which demonstrates the presence of Christ's reconciling power on earth. By its very physical presence as a community, it represents to the world another way of being in the world.

Forms of the Church

In Chapter 5 three proposals were introduced: The first was that the church claims transforming power to change individuals and society. Saving power is communicated by patterns of grace across time and space. The second was that there are six basic patterns of grace, representing the range of ways churches mediate saving power. To review, these six are:

1. Sacramental participation in the community of Christ.

2. Proclamation of the gospel and the response of faith as trust of the heart.

3. Rebirth in the Spirit.

4. Participation in the community of Christ: the gathered church, the disciplined community set apart from the world, or a community of hope in the coming of the Kingdom.

5. Acts of love and justice in response to the call of Christ.

6. Solidarity with Christ who suffers with the oppressed for freedom and justice.

The third proposal was that patterns of grace are the determining factors in the formation of specific traditions. The pattern has formative power because it both organizes the structures and practices in a definite configuration and invests them with specific meaning. But note carefully: a dominant pattern does not deny or exclude the other patterns; rather it gives them different degrees of prominence, not just in terms of their relative value, but also in terms of their daily, weekly, or seasonal practice. For example, all Christians value and practice the Eucharist, but consider the range of meanings and variations in practice. If a dominant pattern does in fact exclude other patterns, it threatens the viability of a tradition by cutting it off from the fullness of the church's life.

The proposal before us is that individual congregations and traditions tend to be formed by these ways of transmitting the gospel. In most cases one or two will dominate, but seldom will all six be equally present in the formation of a tradition. Where would one look to find these formative patterns? If our proposal is correct, one would first look at the primary norm for understanding Christian faith. Then one would proceed to examine how the origin in Christ is remembered, as well as how authority, the goal of history, and strategies for change are defined. Finally, since I have argued that these find visible expression in structures and practices, one would look at the things which organize and sustain the daily life of Christians. Let us proceed to carry out such an analysis of several traditions.

First, if we look at the Roman Catholic tradition, it is clear that the guiding norm is participation in a sacramental community, which maintains its legitimacy by vesting authority in those with direct succession with the apostles. For this community, individuals and the world shall be changed by teaching the true faith and drawing people into the sacramental fellowship of the church. The structures and practices of the church are configured to emphasize this form of the church. As noted earlier, piety is dominated by adoration of the sacrifice of Christ, the saints, and the faithful. The other practices are not denied but shaped by the primary form. For example, spiritual life is structured around participation in the sacraments. Even in the case of solidarity with Christ and the oppressed, Roman Catholics understand this in continuity with the doctrines of Trinity and Incarnation, whereby salvation is expanded to deal with social, economic, and political oppression.

Second, we may use again the example of Lutherans because it is such a good one. If saving power is transmitted by the proclamation of the promise of grace and our response is trust of the heart, then the church must be formed around this central mode of sharing Christ's benefits. Worship must therefore focus on proclamation, as the medieval homily is transformed into a lengthy sermon. But how can believers hear the gospel if it is not read in their own language? The answer is a new translation of the Bible, quickly followed by a new catechism and hymnody. Finally, if baptism is the basis of our vocation or calling to serve God and neighbor, then the distinction of levels of religious life must stop and in its place is set the priesthood of all believers. As with the first example, this primary form for the church does not eliminate the other modes of transmission, but gathers them into this church where they expand the understanding of faith as trust of the heart. Thus Lutherans do not see acts of love and justice as separate from true faith, but the necessary expression of it.

A third example is the Mennonites, which in some ways is more complex in spite of their apparent single mindedness. The dominant norm is the gathered community called out of the world and set apart for the disciplined life of love and reconciliation. In this sense, there is a union of the form of the gathered community with acts of love and justice. Proclamation and faith are of course involved, but mean little if not actualized in participation in a reconciled community (thus the importance of Matthew 18) that is active in works of love (Matt 5–7). The spirituality which emerges from such a form of the church is shaped and strengthened by music (hymns sung in harmony), fellowship, common work, as well as acts of service. In the present situation, the drive to transform the world according to the love of Christ reaches such a high level that one may wonder whether it is appropriate to speak of Mennonites as a sect set apart.

Each of the examples illustrates how a common framework exists within each church: its form is determined by a dominant pattern of grace (mode of transmission) which gives shape and substance to the essential structures and patterns of the community. This process reflects the way the community understands its origin in Jesus Christ and the Spirit, claims authority and looks to the future. Guiding the process is a general norm expressing a vision of Christian faith. In each example, the essential elements have been given specific meaning, which explains how they share a similar structure, claim common things (Bible, sacraments, creed, works of love, etc.) but stand in this world on three separate corners of a town square in such a way that no one would confuse one for another.

The Form of the Church For Our time

Throughout the essay I have attempted to build a case for a theology of the church which is viable for our time. By birth, education, and conviction, I am grounded in a form of the church which takes proclamation and faith as the dominant mode of transmission. Shall then this work conclude with a defense of this traditional Protestant form of the church? It is probably best for the reader to decide how to label the case offered here. Let me simply proceed to propose where I think the church should be in this time.

We have the advantage of living in an ecumenical global village: there is ready access to the breadth of Christian communities in American culture as well as across the world; even more important, we share life with people of other traditions in work, schools, congregations, and family. More is now known about the history of all Christian traditions than ever before. For ecumenical Christians, this means that we have lived for several generations sharing Bible study and theology, liturgies and music, as well as participating in common efforts at witness and service. Thus we find ourselves living in multiple worlds: the names on our churches still identify us with long standing traditions, but our approach to the Bible and theology involves a broad consensus. Moreover, every congregation includes pilgrims and refugees from other denominations as well as stalwart members who can trace their ancestry through one tradition.[9] We

---

9. It is instructive to conduct a bit of grass-roots polling. When you are with a medium size group of members of your congregation, ask them how many were baptized in the denomination of this church? If it is a mainline church in an urban setting, you will be surprised at the response. When I do this the persons baptized from other traditions falls between 30 to 50 percent.

share our lives in families which demonstrate the peace of Christ among old adversaries.

The first thing this means is that there is no going back to the single mindedness of old denominationalism, where one perspective is claimed to be absolutely right and all others are wrong. This does not prevent some from still trying to conduct themselves in this way, but that is not, I believe, the way God is moving us. The time is past for thinking of faithfulness in terms of denominational purity. Stated in positive terms, if we start with a form of the church grounded in proclamation and faith, how can the other five patterns be given more prominence in order to enrich the life of the church, as well as fill in the gaps, omissions, and weaknesses of the traditional Protestant perspective? In one sense this is really not a revolutionary question. As argued above, the other five patterns are already present in Protestant churches, active in organizations within each denomination, present among members of each congregation, and probably carried in the hearts and minds of most pastors. Furthermore, there is nothing in the other five patterns that contradicts the idea that proclamation and the call to faith is a legitimate pattern in the formation of the church. The real question, then, is what would such an inclusive approach look like?

The first three patterns (sacramental, proclamation, and rebirth) share a kinship in pointing to the origin of the church and our own participation in the new life. Each in its own way draws attention to what is received as a gift: baptismal water and Eucharistic bread and wine, the Word proclaimed as promise, and the gift of rebirth by the Spirit. Protestants begin with the pattern of proclamation, but they also celebrate sacramental grace and the gifts of the Spirit. So many structures and practices in the life of the church would be enriched if more attention was given to forming the church as a sacramental fellowship and the practice of spiritual life.

The other three patterns (the gathered community, acts of love and justice, and solidarity with Christ) affirm the way we are united with Christ and live as a community responding to his call. Each of these has also had a major role to play in the traditional Protestant pattern of proclamation. In America, where churches were no longer established as state churches, all churches gave special attention to the gathered community of faith. In this sense, the sixteenth-century distinction between state churches and independent, gathered churches is irrelevant. In the current world of free market religion, all churches must learn the art of persuasion and recognize the serious differences between the gathered community and the world. Likewise, the patterns of engagement with the world (Acts of love and justice and Solidarity) are both present among Protestants. The former has numerous associations with nineteenth-century reform movements, the Social Gospel, and the social activism in the later twentieth century. Solidarity, by contrast, has emerged as a worldwide movement. They differ in one striking respect. In America movements for social justice often tried to unite like-minded people by focusing on the social cause, but omitting references to doctrinal issues, lest the latter divide the participants. By contrast, the pattern of solidarity with Christ arose out of Roman Catholic experience in Latin America and openly appeals to theological themes for motivation and a vision of the future. Thus, while both approaches have drawn Christians together across traditional lines, they have done so in quite different ways.

These brief comments suggest that a unified or inclusive form of the church is quite possible. In fact, it is more than a possibility; it already exists and is coming into being among ecumenical Protestants, as well as Roman Catholics and Anabaptists. It provides for a much richer community life for several reasons: certain structures and practices are strengthened when more attention is given to all patterns of grace in forming the church. For example, worship and education are approached quite differently if one gives more attention to the sacraments and spiritual life, or even the pattern of solidarity with Christ. One of the great benefits of the symbols of baptism and Eucharist is the physical presence of these signs—they exist independent of us, over against us and for us—whether we like it or not. Unlike preaching, which is so dependent on the preacher, the context and our response, the sacraments confront us with the story of Jesus in different ways. The same might be said for governance, evangelism, and fellowship. But the issue before us is not how we create on paper a mosaic of the six patterns, but join them in practice in the life of the church.

The necessity of an inclusive approach becomes evident when we consider what happens when traditions practice a kind of ecclesial single mindedness, where one pattern is overweighted. When this happens the other patterns are minimized or completely eclipsed. Instead of being a guiding principle for organizing the structures and practices of the church, it tends to dominate the life of the church. This in turn means that the long list of structures and practices is reduced to a smaller amount. Three examples readily come to mind:

One example is the concentration on sacramental worship and preservation of traditional doctrine. Traditions which lean in these directions do in fact possess a rich liturgical life, very often connected to faithful pastoral care of members. But the downside of maintaining such practices is often the appearance of a community closed to the modern world, with its emphasis on new knowledge and egalitarian structures. When these traditions defend themselves by means of authoritarian forms of governance, they may further divide and alienate members. They are so convinced that they have the perfect liturgy and doctrine that nothing else really matters.

Another form of concentration is the church as the beloved community. Time, energy, and funds are devoted to sustaining the congregation. When such congregations find themselves in the current cultural setting, where new members are not walking in the door and children are walking out of the door, they are hard pressed because they have not cultivated practices relating to teaching, proclamation, witness, service, and care toward the outside world. Congregations defined as the beloved community also run the risk of being isolated from changes in the larger world, too often resulting in internal conflicts over matters of women's rights, justice, and peace. This in turn accentuates the loss of younger generations, which perceive the church as locked into the past. In its extreme form, the beloved community becomes a family chapel, sustained by a limited number of inter-locking families which make a commitment to continue.

A final example is the concentration on social witness and action in the pursuit of justice and peace, to the point where ministries required for sustaining the gathered community are ignored. Over time this means a decrease of time, staff, and resources to ministries of worship, education, the call of ordained leaders, the nurture of pastors and congregations, stewardship and evangelism. What should also be noted is that when this concentration occurs, all other ministries tend to be redefined in terms of issues of social justice. The result of such practice is the decline in membership, giving, and the number of new ordinands, as well as a general division between those advocating for the church as a social witness and those advocating for a broader ecclesiology. When this split is between national offices and congregations, there is a general fracture. The embrace of the form of the church as social witness has eclipsed a commitment to a more inclusive ecclesiology because the church is defined as the social agenda.

In all three examples, the concentration on only one or two structures and practices creates a de-emphasis on others, even to the point of a void. If one is troubled by the contraction of the church's life in these three ways, one could argue that such concerns should have been raised in earlier chapters when dealing with basic norms and Christological considerations. Why wait until this chapter, dealing with the church's structures and practices, to protest against dysfunctional forms of the church? My first response is that appeals to general theological norms have been made, with little success. But a more important response is that the approach taken here insists on raising the question of ecclesiology. If one examines the list of structures and practices which embody the fullness of the church's life (see the Sixth Essential Component), how can one possible argue that one aspect of the church is the only one that counts? It is precisely in this context that the full meaning of what was said before is made clear: the church is more than Word and Sacrament, it is more than the gathering of the beloved community, and it is more than the social agenda. Ecclesiology is not simply an after thought, a utilitarian infrastructure needed to get on to other things. It is the way the church embodies the new life in Christ.

Faithfulness and Viability

Once one has defined the church it is appropriate to ask: What does it mean to be faithful in our time? Since I have tried to show why and how traditions vary in their faith and life, one obvious answer would be to call all Christians to be faithful to the gospel as each tradition embodies it. Patterns of grace are strategies for changing individuals and society according to the commission of Christ. But how do communities keep forms of grace focused on their intended purpose? How do these forms continue to function boldly as words of judgment and grace—against the world and the church? The first answer is to remember what they are: gifts from God which have transforming power to change individuals and the world. They enable the church to be an agent of mission, demonstrating the reality of new life. If they are effective, it is because God is working through them. Our responsibility, however, is to be faithful to the calling given to us: to give our minds and hearts as best we can to engage in these acts and to hold one another responsible for faithful use.

The willingness to affirm the validity of multiple patterns of grace, forming many traditions, however, presents us with a challenge. It is certainly one which arises only in a time such as ours. This is the challenge and the gift of grace for our time: to open our minds and hearts to alternative patterns of grace. In this sense, faithfulness must not be defined solely in terms of loyalty of one's own form of the church, but the courage to incorporate other forms. As we have already discovered, the gain is far greater than the loss: individual structures and practices have become richer as we encounter the fullness of saving power. The recognition of other patterns of Christian life does not negate our own, but usually leads to greater clarity as to what specifically is the gift in our own tradition. Such openness also frees us from the need to be dogmatic and compulsive about our own practices, as if the value of one tradition depended upon being the only right one. My tradition is not diminished by affirming the validity of other forms of the church. When I am overwhelmed by Russian Orthodox or Black Gospel music, my Germanic Protestant heart is expanded.

In this final part, we shall explore the meaning of faithfulness as openness to the fullness of grace in the whole church. This is not the only form of faithfulness. It certainly does not speak to all the specific crises churches face. But it is in our time an overriding issue which will affect the viability of the church for several generations.

The Practice of Repentance

Of *The 95 Theses* Martin Luther nailed to the church door, the first deserves regular attention: "When our Lord and Master, Jesus Christ, said 'Repent,' He called for the entire life of believers to be one of penitence." [10] Thinking about a more inclusive church requires a spirit of repentance to keep our own traditions viable and to keep our minds open to other traditions. Some will argue that we are most likely to reach out to others when our own tradition has lost its fire. No doubt there are examples of this. But

10. Cf. *Martin Luther: Selections From His Writings*, 490.

it is just as likely that when our own practices lose their intended purpose, we still cling to them and become defensive. In such a state, we are even more likely to be threatened by the gifts of grace from other traditions. Why else are creative changes resisted with such vehemence?

Our own practices are always in danger of becoming routine. We can read Scripture, pray and recite the liturgy without much thought, as if they were all background music. The patterns of our lives thus redefine these religious acts rather than having them define our lives. This may be called the domestication of the forms of grace. Strategies for changing lives are converted into systems for short term aid. The sacraments become only assurances of God's love, preaching only parcels out bits of meaning, advice and approval, acts of love become charity, and the Spirit's power is offered as a means for self-help. In effect, all of the forms of grace turn from what God is doing in the world to the short range needs of the institutional church and its members. They cease to be strategies pointing to the unfolding Rule of God and instead become remedies to solve personal problems. When this happens they are co-opted by what I have called the American Cultural Religion, where God is perceived as the One who meets our needs and religion is all about me.

For example, to allow baptism to become only a naming ceremony, void of its dramatic implications for change, is to convert it into a cultural rite of passage. To preach little sermons, which describe the historical context of a text and share small bits of meaning for our lives, void of any reference to how the text fits into God's intention to change the world, is to settle for small-scale religion that we can control. Even the alternative of preaching big, dramatic sermons based on captivating stories can miss the point if the stories do not turn us to God's larger purposes. Big stories may capture our attention for seventeen minutes, but what is the lasting impact on Monday morning? To be sure, the forms of grace have transforming power only if God wills it. And it must also be said that God can and will use our efforts in spite of their frailty. But these facts do not absolve us from using forms of grace as they were intended to be used: gifts of God to transform lives.

But what is the alternative to allowing our practices to become routine? One is to begin reading Scripture in a new way. We traditionally ask of Scripture two questions: What does the text mean? What does it mean for me? On the surface, these are good questions and can be the catalysts for hearing the gospel. But they too easily limit the text by expecting it to speak to my perspective and needs. As a consequence, we need to ask two additional questions in order to break out of the limits set by our culture. The first is: Why do we resist this text? The second is: What would happen if the good news found in the text was used to reform the church? Both of these questions push us to read Scripture in new ways. Let us consider each:

Every major passage of Scripture challenges us to think in new ways. But we resist doing so. We will not be able to hear the good news unless we acknowledge that we do not want to be changed. For example, in the parable of the prodigal son, Jesus builds our resistance into the parable itself. After depicting the unimaginable love of God in the father's open embrace of his rebellious son, we are confronted with the older brother. The brother represents our resistance to the idea of unmerited grace, which turns upside down our world of legality, balance of payments, and punishment of sinners. The fact is, we don't like this parable and we will not be able to like it until we deal at length with our resistance to it. But sometimes the resistance is not in the text and we have to discover it. For example, a pastor conducted a Bible study on the parable of Lazarus at the rich man's gate. Day after day the rich man never saw the poor man. Without prompting, one member of the study group asked: "Why don't we see the poor?" Here was the question of resistance and it completely changed the reading of the text.

Now consider the impact of the last question: What would happen if the church practiced seeing the poor? We are suddenly out of the realm of what does the text mean to me and have moved to the realm where the church as a community is being formed by the text. The text is not simply for preachers or individual readers; it is for the formation of the church according to the calling of Christ to be agents of reconciliation in the world.

This approach to the reading of Scripture suggests that preaching needs to become a process of double discovery. As we struggle with our resistance to a text, we first discover that what we bring to the text regarding ourselves and God is too often biased if not false. But emerging from the text is a more honest and hopeful view of ourselves as well as of God. This cannot happen unless we are confronted with our illusions of innocence and self-righteousness, which are the very things prompting us to resist a gospel of grace and holiness. Just as the old self must die in order for the new self to be reborn, so the old god of our childhood, the god who assures material comfort or the god of the nation who condones our supremacy—these gods must die so that we may put our trust in the God of Jesus Christ.

Reading with an eye for our resistance, or preaching and listening for discovery, however, are not three-step techniques. They require imagination, an openness to the Spirit, and a willingness to try new things. The well known prayers used for confessions of sin are rich in meaning. It gives one pause to consider things we have done—known and unknown—or the evil done on our behalf. It is hard to quarrel with such language, as long as it is not so well known that we glide over it without knowing what we are saying. There is also the real possibility that in a culture so saturated with defensiveness, many will have no idea what is meant by such language. In such a situation, care needs to be given to finding words that allow us to see ourselves as we are. Toward this goal it might be helpful to move the confession of sin after the reading of Scripture and the sermon—the very things which have the potential to break our protective defenses and allow us to see ourselves as God would have us be. The confession of sin is not an entrance fee paid right after the first hymn, five minutes into the service, nor is it a magical cure. It ought to represent the earnest struggle between our resistance and what God is doing for us in Jesus Christ.

It hardly needs saying that Luther's first thesis would prompt us to read Scripture and pray at all meetings of the community, not just on Sunday. Such practice would elevate all aspects of community life, as well as open up new possibilities for spiritual life in the congregation.

When Christians speak of salvation, it is often symbolized by the breaking down of barriers, the end of warfare and the gathering of all things into the peace of Christ. But in actual fact, Christian communities are reflections of the limits set by race, language, political and class distinctions. In such a situation, the practice of repentance might mean finding ways to meet the future Christ brings: How can we come face to face with our opposites? Whether this would involve travel to the opposites, or welcoming guests, or speaking in positive ways about opposites (in a high-tech world such speech could also involve visual presentations), congregations could protest against themselves and resist their own resistance. What would it mean to encounter other people of different class, race, language, or age? Who do we have in mind when we speak of "them" in neutral or negative tones? Who is most unlike the members of our congregation? In our known world, who is the most unknown? Repentance means that we do not have to accept our isolation. We can find ways to open ourselves to grow in our faithfulness.

An Inclusive Spirituality

Protestants were usually caught off guard by questions about spirituality, especially if this refers to the many forms practiced by Roman Catholics. Nor did the popular forms of spirituality, found in bestsellers, reflect the Protestant heritage. These books usually encouraged readers to explore their inner thoughts, locate God in themselves, with an eye toward self-improvement. But I have always felt that there is a unique form of Protestant spirituality. It has to do with preparing to receive the gifts of God and celebrating the gifts given. For this reason such spirituality has always focused on reading Scripture, individual and communal prayer, and preaching, which proclaims the promise and invites a response of trust. It alternates between remembrance (the story of Jesus' life, death, and resurrection) and hope (asking what God is doing in the world). There is a need to journey inward in order to deal with our resistance and turning to God. But it has never emphasized spiritual exercises akin to classic Roman Catholic spirituality or more current practices of contemplation because the source of new life is not in us but in Christ. In many ways this is exemplified by the Protestant love of music, especially hymnody. It is music which wakes us up, pierces the heart, and elevates us to a higher level. This latter point is especially the case with harmony that is only achieved by two or more voices singing together. Harmony is a symbol of the reconciliation of solitary voices into some thing which they can not create by themselves. Anyone who has heard Mennonites sing hymns and their glorious Doxology can testify to the power of such music to elevate the individual to the joy of communal life.

But having sung the praises of Protestant spirituality, how can we open ourselves to multiple forms of spiritual life? Of course, this is already happening as we share liturgical and spiritual practices and musical traditions. This has produced so much sharing of ideas and practices that it is difficult to unravel the origins of many liturgies, the contents of new hymnals or communal practices. We borrow liturgies, prayers, liturgical robes, hymns, and ways of speaking because they appear to be grace-filled. What is less stated is that we make changes because certain practices of our own have simply run dry. For example, there obviously was a point for Zwingli's radical cleansing of the great church in Zurich, or the Puritan insistence on simplicity of architectural style. But at what point does one finally admit that one has been living in a rather austere and barren religious landscape, or that the gifts of color, symbol, art, and contrasts of light and darkness might be forms of grace? In one sense, conservatives who resist any change or new idea are correct: such things may threaten the purity of traditional practices. But there is also the possibility that changes and new ideas might also enrich and/or assist us in reviving the original meaning of the very traditions we wish to conserve. The music from all of the major traditions has the power to achieve the goals mentioned above. For this reason each tradition needs to nurture its own music as well as engage in mutual sharing.

Most traditions have recognized the need to be inclusive in our worship by paying attention to the church year. Not only do we have the great festivals, with their elaborate symbols, music, and practices, to remind us of the fullness of the gospel, but we also have the cycle of Scripture readings which require us to move beyond favorite texts. In our time the use of a common lectionary and celebration of common festivals has been a great opportunity for sharing among different traditions. The more we enthusiastically engage in such common practices the more we discover new ways to be faithful.

One way to bring different traditions together is by opening the liturgy of the Eucharist to a wider range of theological affirmations and the varied moments in the life of the community. In general, liturgies for the Eucharist concentrate on sin, guilt, and forgiveness. As I have argued, forgiveness is a major form of saving power but not the only one (e.g., consider the ideas of liberation, reconciliation and the restoration of God's purpose). While current liturgies never intended this to occur, the fact is that this service points us back to the death of Christ and focuses primarily on the forgiveness of sins. This is further complicated by the American tendency to understand forgiveness as absolution for individual sins—not social, political, or economic sins. To be sure, current liturgies are loaded with references to themes other than individual forgiveness, but usually in the briefest manner. As a result, we do not celebrate the fullness of the gospel with one or two liturgies printed in our worship books. Nor do we celebrate and/or minister to the wide range of human needs with the standard service. Why would one use the same Eucharistic liturgy at a youth retreat, a wedding, a funeral, or a gathering of congregational leaders? Why should liturgies for Advent, Epiphany, Lent, and Easter all be the same?[11] But if multiple liturgies were created for quite specific purposes, it is possible that the Eucharist would become again one of the central ways of uniting persons across traditions. For example, if we had liturgies to celebrate the goodness of the earth (including a call to repentance for our abuse of it), or solidarity of Christ with those who suffer, or the peace of Christ in a violent world, then the Eucharist might be the rightful meeting place for the church gathered and scattered. It also might be the opportunity for those gathered at the table to see the Eucharist as it was meant to be: the celebration of our unity with Christ in the present as we seek to serve Christ.

There are other patterns and rhythms that enable us to be attentive to what is happening to people. There are the four seasons of the year and the seasons of life. There is the rhythm of work, rest, and renewal which takes place on a daily basis, over a week or even a year. Giving attention to the sick, the dying and the grieving opens our eyes to many needs. But shall a congregation be attentive only to these rhythms among its own members, their relatives, or others in the community? It will not take long before someone asks whether the church should just be offering acts of charity or should it address larger problems affecting the health and welfare of people. There really is no end to the way that attention to real needs becomes the occasion for mission, if we only stop to look at what is happening. On any Sunday morning there is much to celebrate, but there is also much to cause sorrow and concern. Most of this is too easily

11. For nearly a decade I have worked with pastors on a project to expand the number of Eucharistic liturgies. These efforts produced several liturgies for Epiphany and Lent, each giving special attention to the respective season. In addition to focusing on a theme, the effort also took another step. It broke down the barrier between the so-called regular service and the Eucharist, usually added on at the end. What emerged was a unified liturgy, which announced the theme at the beginning, moved through prayers, Scripture, and sermon so that the Eucharist was the culmination of the entire worship service. What was especially noteworthy was that lay people saw immediately what was happening: that Eucharist was incorporated into the service and the entire service had one over-riding theme.

lost when we never get beyond the initial formal greeting, or even worse, expect that everyone should be happy!

The ecumenical movement has expanded the understanding of worship and the spiritual life for most Protestants. Many Protestants have incorporated many practices from Roman Catholic spirituality. For low-church Protestants, these developments have enriched worship as we recover the use of art, symbol, light/darkness, and incorporate new music. But there is much still to be done: reaching out to young people and several generations of alienated adults; finding creative solutions to congregational music wars, creating ways to inspire and nourish witness and service in the world; crossing the barriers of class, race, and language.

The Marks of Vitality

For at least two generations there has been a quest for The Magic Answer—the thing that will solve the church's problems and/or cause it to grow and be a vital force in the world. All manner of organizational strategies, technological changes, and special programs have been proposed. The high membership, fast growing churches have been described in detail. More than one congregation has tried to emulate the new cathedrals of success, or even the anti-cathedrals claiming to appeal to the disaffected. Likewise, a variety of images for ordained ministry have dominated annual meetings, conferences and of course, seminary education. As this essay comes to a close, what counsel can be offered to those who care and love the church? There is a message here, but it is modest one, calling us to affirm that Christ has given the gift and promise of new life to the church. It is time to get back to basics: to embrace the church as the community of Christ called to represent grace and holiness in this world. Even in the midst of a world in perpetual crisis, now is the time to love and care for the church.

The distinctive task of this essay has been to argue that faithfulness to Christ necessarily involves an affirmation of the church. We have come to new life in and through the community of Christ; our vision for a world of peace is born of the Spirit in and through the community of Christ. But it is not easy to say these things or for people in and outside the church to hear them. Some churches claim too much regarding truth and power, casting doubt about all claims for the church. Some believers, in and outside of churches, want to follow Christ but have no patience for churches. Their zeal for righteousness excludes concern for the care of the church as a community over time in this world. If the one side gives us negative images of the church, the other side suggests by inaction that the church is unnecessary. The burden of the essay, therefore, has been to set forth a viable and comprehensive definition of the church for our time. If there is any merit in this, then it follows that the marks of vitality for churches will point to the faithfulness of churches to be Christ's community of new life in our time.

The first mark of vitality is present when churches affirm and embody the fullness of the community's life. Here I refer simply to the basic argument of the essay: the church is best defined in a comprehensive way as a community existing in time and space. It has essential components that define its life: the remembrance of its origin, norms, claims to authority, hope for the future, strategies of grace, and communal life. Not one of these may be short changed or excluded without threatening the church's vitality. The church also embodies the new life of Christ in many structures and practices which are most often called forms of ministry. Good things happen when churches pay attention to all of these ministries: worship and social witness, fellowship and education, the interaction of sacraments, preaching and music, evangelism and the care of members, stewardship and service to others. And yes, churches need a place to gather out of the rain, where all the ministries may be embodied and nurtured.

There is a definite synergism that arises when all of these things are embodied in a church. Not only are a variety of needs and callings affirmed, but each of the parts of the church is strengthened in unexpected ways when there is a vision for the whole church. By contrast, churches lose vitality when they insist that the church is only the sacraments or preaching, only fellowship for the faithful, only attending to a social agenda. The first mark of vitality, therefore, is the willingness to affirm the church as the community of new life in Christ, with all of its components, structures, and practices. It is in these things that we prove our faithfulness.

A second mark of vitality for our time lies in the willingness to engage in the interchange between the patterns of grace that have formed individual churches. The reason for this is clear: if all six patterns of grace affirm something that is valid—with respect to faithfulness to Christ and representing the gospel to the world—then we can no longer continue in isolation from other patterns. In fact, to press on in isolation, still defining vitality as faithfulness only to one's own form of the church, will probably mean a loss of vitality. The fact is that congregations already have a spread of members who gravitate toward the different patterns. The same can be said for those outside the church: some seek the experience of the sacred, others seek genuine community, while others seek to transcend themselves in service. Churches that continue to practice an ecclesial single mindedness will not meet the needs of their own members or those outside the church. The second mark of vitality, therefore, will prompt churches to risk embracing the gifts given to many forms of the church. It will call them to use these gifts to strengthen the community of Christ—because it is a good thing for brothers and sisters to dwell in unity. It will call them to witness to the new life of Christ in the world—because it was ultimately for this purpose that the Word became incarnate.

Bibliography

Aulen, Gustav. *Christus Victor: An Historical Study of the Three Main Types of the Idea of the Atonement.* Translated by A. G. Hebert. London: S.P.C.K., 1931.

Bartlett, Anthony W. *Cross Purposes: The Violent Grammar of Christian Atonement.* Harrisburg, PA: Trinity, 2001.

Borg, Marcus. *Meeting Jesus Again for the First Time: The Historical Jesus and the Heart of Contemporary Faith.* New York: Harper Collins, 1994.

Calvin, John. *The Institutes of the Christian Religion.* Edited by John T. McNeill and translated by Ford Lewis Battles. Vol. 20 of *The Library of Christian Classics*, edited by John Baillie, John T. McNeill, and Henry P. Van Dusen. Philadelphia: Westminster, 1960.

Carey, Greg. *Elusive Apocalypse: Reading Authority in the Revelation to John.* Macon, GA: Mercer University Press, 1999.

Carroll, Jack. *As One With Authority: Reflective Leadership in Ministry.* Louisville: Westminster/John Knox, 1991.

Carter, Stephen. *The Culture of Disbelief: How American Law and Politics Trivialize Religious Devotion.* New York: Harper Collins, 1993.

Catechism of the Catholic Church: With Modifications from the Editio Typic. New York: Image Books, Doubleday, 1995.

Crossan, Dominic John. *Jesus, a Revolutionary Biography.* New York: Harper Collins, 1994.

Dulles, Avery. *Models of the Church*, Expanded ed. New York: Doubleday, 1987.

Gonzalez, Justo L. *The Early Church to the Dawn of the Reformation.* Vol. I of *The Story of Christianity.* New York: Harper Collins, 1984.

Gutierrez, Gustavo. *A Theology of Liberation.* Translated and edited by Caridad Inda and John Eagleson. Revised ed. Maryknoll, NY: Orbis, 1973.

The Heidelberg Catechism: A New Translation for the 21st Century. Translated by Lee Barrett, III. Cleveland: The Pilgrim Press, 2007.

Heim, S. Mark. *Saved From Sacrifice: A Theology of the Cross.* Grand Rapids: Eerdmans, 2006.

Hudson, Winthrop S. *Religion in America.* New York: Scribner's, 1965.

Hunter, James Davison. *Culture Wars: The Struggle to Define America.* New York: Harper Collins, 1991.

Irenaeus, "Against Heresies," *The Apostolic Fathers with Justin Martyr and Irenaeus.* Edited by A. Cleveland Coxe. Vol. I of *The Ante-Nicene Fathers: Translations of the Writings of the Fathers Down to A.D. 325.* Edited by Alexander Roberts and James Donaldson. New York: Scribner's, 1985.

Leith, John H, editor. *Creeds of the Churches.* Third ed. Louisville: Westminster John Knox, 1982.

Littlejohn, W. Bradford. *The Mercersburg Theology and the Quest for Reformed Catholicity.* Eugene, OR: Pickwick, 2009.

Luther, Martin. "The Freedom of a Christian." In *Martin Luther: Selections from His Writings.* Edited by John Dillenberger. Garden City, NY: Doubleday, 1961.

———. *The Large Catechism of Martin Luther.* Translated by Robert H. Fischer. Philadelphia: Fortress, 1959.

———. "The Ninety-Five Theses, 1517." In *Martin Luther: Selections From His Writings.* Edited by John Dillenberger. Garden City, NY: Doubleday, 1961.

———. "On the Councils and the Church (1539)." In *Church and Ministry III,* edited by Eric W. Gritsch and translated by Charles M. Jacobs, revised by Eric W. Gritsch. Vol. 41 of Luther's Works, edited by Helmut T. Lehmann. Philadelphia: Fortress, 1966.

———. "Two Kinds of Righteousness." In *Martin Luther: Selections from His Writings.* Edited by John Dillenberger. Garden City, NY: Doubleday, 1961.

Meyendorff, John. *Catholicity and the Church.* Crestwood, NY: St. Vladimir's Seminary Press, 1983.

Nevin, John Williamson. "The Anxious Bench." In *Catholic and Reformed: Selected Theological Writings of John Williamson Nevin.* Edited by Charles Yrigoyen, Jr. and George H. Bricker. Pittsburgh: Pickwick, 1978.

Nevin, John Williamson. *The Mystical Presence.* Edited by Bard Thompson and George H. Bricker. Lancaster Series on the Mercersburg Theology; IV. Philadelphia: United Church Press, 1966.

Niebuhr, H. Richard. *Christ and Culture.* New York: Harper, 1951.

———. "The Grace of Doing Nothing." *Christian Century* (March 23, 1932) 378–80.

———. *The Kingdom of God in America.* New York: Harper and Row, 1937.

———. "The Only Way into the Kingdom of God." *Christian Century* (April 6, 1932) 447.

Sanders, E. P. *The Historical Figure of Jesus.* London: Penguin, 1993.

Schaff, Phillip. *The Principle of Protestantism.* Philadelphia: United Church Press, 1964.

Schmiechen, Peter. *Saving Power: Theories of Atonement and Forms of the Church.* Grand Rapids: Eerdmans, 2005.

———. *Christ the Reconciler: A Theology for Opposites, Differences, and Enemies.* Grand Rapids: Eerdmans, 1996.

Silone, Ignazio. *Bread and Wine,* Translated by Harvey Fergusson, II. New York: New American Library, 1963.

Stringfellow, William. *A Private and Public Faith.* Grand Rapids: Eerdmans, 1962.

Tertullian. *Treatises on Penance.* Translated by William P. LeSaint. Vol. XXVIII of *Ancient Christian Writers: The Works of the Fathers in Translation.* Edited by Johannes Quasten and Walter J. Burghardt. Westminster, MD: Newman, 1959.

Volf, Miroslav. *Exclusion and Embrace.* Nashville: Abingdon, 1996.

Walker,Waliston, et al. *A History of the Christian Church.* Fourth ed. New York: Charles Scribner's Sons, 1985.

Webster's New World Dictionary of the American Language. Cleveland: The World Publishing Co., 1956.

Welch, Claude. *The Reality of the Church.* New York: Scribner's, 1958.

28225295R00109

Made in the USA
Lexington, KY
16 December 2013